Praise for *Love on Ev[ery]*

"As a Catholic Sister, I found Lama Pal[den's] *[Love on Every] Breath*, to be an important spiritual v[...] [...] spiritual tradition. Living in such a tim[e of ...] violence, Palden's sharing of how to grow our capacity for compassion through her enhanced practice of Tonglen is so needed. Her explanation of the Buddhist framework for this practice is clear and interspersed with examples from her life, making it very readable for those not as familiar with that tradition."

— **Sister Nancy Sylvester,**
IHM, Institute for Communal Contemplation and Dialogue

"*Love on Every Breath* illuminates a clear and practical pathway for cultivating an awakened, loving heart. Drawing deeply from her Buddhist training and life experiences, Lama Palden Drolma masterfully presents a powerful guide for navigating the painful world we live in with compassion, openness, and healing. This book is an invaluable contribution for our times."

— **Wendy Garling,** author of *Stars at Dawn:*
Forgotten Stories of Women in the Buddha's Life

"With *Love on Every Breath*, Lama Palden offers an accessible and adaptable method to transmute suffering — our own and others' — and to more deeply attune with our inherent loving awareness. An important, illuminating, and timely contribution!"

— **John J. Prendergast, PhD,** author of
The Deep Heart and *In Touch*

"*Love on Every Breath* by Lama Palden Drolma brings to the public an ancient meditation practice, one that can help transform our personal and collective grief by awakening the love and compassion that are inherent in all beings. This book is a beautiful exploration of a practice that is so very needed today and is accessible to all. It is a practice that can be done in solitude in deep meditation or on the subway during one's daily commute. As individuals and as a collective, we are dealing with much suffering in our world today, both human and planetary. There is no more urgent task than to learn to transform this pain into love so that we can awaken to a greater sense of well-being and to the true reality of what is. Lama Palden shows us the way by recounting stories from her own journey. She shows us that by practicing the Love on Every Breath meditation techniques, we, too, can find the beauty and love that reside in each and every heart."

— **Dena Merriam,** founder of the Global Peace Initiative of Women and the Contemplative Alliance

"As the rising voice of the feminine gives new life to perennial wisdom teachings, hidden jewels are being revealed through a feminine lens and rendering the esoteric utterly available. Tonglen is such a treasure. Through Lama Palden's loving heart and lucid mind, we are offered practical tools with which to take the pain of the world all the way in, where it may be transmuted into a healing elixir for all beings."

— **Mirabai Starr,** author of *Caravan of No Despair* and *Wild Mercy*

"The Tibetan Buddhist practice of Tonglen — breathing in suffering and breathing out compassion — is a once-secret treasure that our world now urgently needs. Lama Palden faithfully transmits the traditional instruction she received from her many Tibetan masters, while speaking in the warm, conversational tone of an intimate friend. The book is liberally sprinkled with striking tales of her own years of study in India and Nepal....*Love on Every Breath* is rigorous enough to appeal to the dedicated Buddhist practitioner, while being accessible to people of every religious or nonreligious persuasion."

— **Lewis Richmond,** author of *Aging as a Spiritual Practice*

"Drawing on Eastern spirituality and modern psychology, *Love on Every Breath* offers a tried-and-true method for living joyfully in a suffering world. Indeed, this empowering book reveals how we can transform ourselves and our world by opening our hearts to others. If you want to bring more kindness into the world, read this book."

— **Christine Carter, PhD,** author of *Raising Happiness* and *The Sweet Spot: How to Accomplish More by Doing Less*

Love on Every Breath

Love *on* Every Breath

*Tonglen Meditation for
Transforming Pain into Joy*

LAMA PALDEN DROLMA

Foreword by Sylvia Boorstein

New World Library
Novato, California

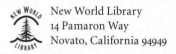 New World Library
14 Pamaron Way
Novato, California 94949

The material in this book is intended for education. It is not meant to take the place of diagnosis and treatment by a qualified medical practitioner or therapist. No expressed or implied guarantee of the effects of the use of the recommendations can be given or liability taken.

All names have been changed to protect privacy.

Text design by Tona Pearce Myers

Library of Congress Cataloging-in-Publication Data

Names: Drolma, Palden, Lama, [date]– author.
Title: Love on every breath : Tonglen meditation for transforming pain into
    joy / by Lama Palden Drolma.
Description: Novato, California : New World Library, [2019].
Identifiers: LCCN 2018052576 (print) | LCCN 2019000005 (ebook) |
    ISBN 9781608685776 (e-book) | ISBN 9781608685769 (print : alk. paper) |
    ISBN 9781608685776 (ebk.)
Subjects: LCSH: Meditation--Buddhism. | Spiritual life--Buddhism. |
    Compassion--Religious aspects--Buddhism. | Buddhism--China--Tibet
    Autonomous Region.
Classification: LCC BQ5620 (ebook) | LCC BQ5620 .D76 2019 (print) |
    DDC 294.3/4435--dc23
LC record available at https://lccn.loc.gov/2018052576

First printing, May 2019
ISBN 978-1-60868-576-9
Ebook ISBN 978-1-60868-577-6
Printed in Canada on 100% postconsumer-waste recycled paper

 New World Library is proud to be a Gold Certified Environmentally
Responsible Publisher. Publisher certification awarded by Green
Press Initiative.

10   9   8   7   6   5   4   3   2   1

I dedicate this book to Kalu Rinpoche, my beloved teacher, innovator, who gave us the priceless jewels of the Dharma, and gave us the love, support, and skills to actualize awakening. And to our human family — may we learn to be kind with one another and ourselves, honor our equality, and cooperate in order to face our challenges.

Contents

Foreword

*I*n 2005, I was one of two thousand attendees at a weeklong teaching given by His Holiness the Dalai Lama in Tucson, Arizona. The text for the course was chapter 6 of the Guide to the Bodhisattva's Way of Life written by the sixth-century Buddhist teacher Shantideva. Chapter 6 is entitled "Patience." His Holiness read, then translated, then commented on each verse as if it were freshly new and intriguing, even as I was thinking that each verse reiterated the same message: Whatever happens that might arouse negative energy in your mind, expand your perspective so that kindness and compassion is your response. I did also notice that the mood of the room, and my own mood, seemed to become more and more exalted as the week passed, as if we were sharing a space of unshakable benevolence. After His Holiness had read the last verse, he suddenly put his head down between his hands and leaned forward in his seat. When he straightened up, and used his handkerchief to wipe his eyes, we could see that he had been crying.

It was lunchtime of the final day of the conference. We had one more session scheduled for the afternoon. His Holiness then said, "This afternoon we'll have a bodhisattva vow ceremony. Does anyone have any questions about that?"

A man very far in the back of the room stood up and said, "I am a devout Catholic. Do you think it is okay for me to participate in that initiation?" His Holiness paused for a brief moment and then said, "I think it's okay."

We adjourned for lunch and then reassembled in our pre-assigned seats for the final session. Everyone stood up as the Dalai Lama entered, did three full-prostration bows before the Buddha image, and took his seat. I imagined, as I thought everyone did, that he would begin the bodhisattva vow instructions. Instead, he looked to the back of the room where the prelunch question had come from. "I've been reflecting more," he said, "about whether a person who was committed to another religious path should take bodhisattva initiation. And I'm quite sure it is okay. After all," he concluded, "compassion is compassion and a blessing is a blessing."

The Tucson conference thirteen years ago still resonates in my mind for what I understand as its two main conclusions. The first, the one that comes when I think of His Holiness's tears, is the truth that a fully loving heart is the fundamental source of liberation from suffering and of happiness. The second is the recognition, across traditions, that the point and the promise of spiritual practice is developing the human capacity to respond to suffering with wisdom and benevolence.

Love on Every Breath is another translation, interpretation, and presentation of an ancient meditation. In its own way, it moves systematically through all the impediments, the habits of mind and heart, that block the wholehearted expression of love. Lama Palden's perspective — that of a contemporary Western woman raised in a loving, Christian family who found the fullest expression of her spirituality in the Tibetan Buddhist tradition as a devotee of the venerable Kalu Rinpoche and then as a teacher in two lineages — provides a smooth bridge for today's seekers to access these teachings. I am particularly heartened to have this book become available right now, at a time when the level of suffering of the world on every level, from global to personal, cannot be ignored. My hope is that it might soothe the hearts of everyone who reads it and encourage them to manifest and teach the possibility of the healing potential of love to everyone around them.

Sylvia Boorstein
October 2018

Preface

*T*his book teaches a meditation, a spiritual practice, that I call Love on Every Breath. This meditation opens the heart to uncover our innate awakened love and wisdom and allow it to thrive, so we can blossom into who we truly are and share our unique gifts and presence with the world. It strengthens our love for ourselves, for those close to us, for those we come in contact with, and for everyone — each and every being on this planet and beyond.

Many of us take in the suffering of others, and it simply sits in us, unprocessed, weighing us down. Love on Every Breath provides a way to transform this pain into love and joy.

We have been given the capacity to love and to think, reason, intuit, and find solutions. Love is what humanity now desperately needs. If we can open our hearts to ourselves and to all others, we can heal our human family. We have the capacity to solve all our problems, but it requires love. Love moves us forward. Love is caring. Love leads to cooperation.

This meditation can be done "on-the-spot" in daily life as

well as on the cushion, and I provide instructions for both. When we engage with the meditation, love reveals the innate beauty of our hearts. Healing our own wounding and suffering with love gives us the capacity to be present with and truly love others. As we heal, our innate goodness, our innate wisdom and love, comes into the forefront of our consciousness and infuses our speech and actions.

I offer you this practice in the spirit of sharing this thousand-year-old meditation from the lineage of the dakinis Niguma and Sukhasiddhi. May all beings come to happiness and peace!

Part One

THE GROUND

Love and Compassion

At the core of hope is a leap of faith — not that it will all come out right, but a faith that holds that what we do matters. How it will come to matter, who it will come to inspire, what positive effect it will have — is not ours to know.

— RABBI DAVID COOPER

*L*ove on Every Breath is an ancient Tibetan Buddhist Vajrayana* meditation from the Shangpa lineage that combines breath, awareness, imagination, and an energetic transformation process. The meditation brings all these components together in a powerful way in order to open our

---

* Vajrayana, from Sanskrit, is the actual term for Tibetan Buddhism. *Vajra* means "indestructible" or "diamond" and refers to our indestructible diamond-like true nature that is undisturbed by birth and death. *Yana* means "vehicle," which means a vehicle or path that takes us to enlightenment. There are three primary *yanas* in Buddhism: Theravadin, Mahayana (which includes Zen and Chan), and Vajrayana.

hearts, to reveal and cultivate our kindness, love, compassion, and wisdom. In Tibetan, this is called the Extraordinary Tonglen, since it uses special techniques of Vajrayana to transform suffering. The Tibetan word *tonglen* is composed of two words — *tong* means "giving or sending," and *len* means "receiving or taking." First, we open ourselves to receive and feel the suffering of ourselves and others, breathing it into our heart center. This is the "taking." The suffering is then instantaneously and effortlessly liberated in the heart and transformed by a special method into unconditional love. At this point, on the out-breath, love and healing energy are sent back out to whomever you are doing the meditation for at the moment, whether yourself or another. This is the "sending."

The primary purpose of the Love on Every Breath meditation is to cultivate our love and compassion, to transform and liberate our heart. When we come from a place of love, everything shifts for us. This book gives you the tools to transform and empower yourself and come to a place of creative engaged freedom.

The Love on Every Breath meditation is not an exotic Himalayan practice, but it is something that emerges out of us spontaneously and naturally. It is inherent in us to want to remove suffering — others' or our own. The problem for many children (and adults) is that we absorb the suffering of others, and then it stagnates inside of us. Love on Every Breath gives a way for the suffering to be liberated in the body and the psyche and emerge as compassion. There is a felt sense as this happens.

A Story of a Healing

Ever since I was young, I've felt that there has to be something beneath the surface of daily life, something more real, more true than what I see and experience around me. I wanted to connect with this deeper truth. My first memory of church was when I was three. I had on my good winter coat, and I was delighted with a new fur muff that was keeping my hands warm and cozy. As I walked up to the church with my family in the brisk air of a gray winter day, I remember thinking, *Maybe this is the place where people are more real.* I was raised as an Episcopalian, and I loved the church. I felt the blessing of the Holy Trinity during Holy Communion, and this sense of blessing only increased as the years went by. The primary teaching I received in church was that Jesus's message is love: Everyone is loved by God, and all are God's children. In hindsight, this pointed to the basic goodness and equality of everyone.

As a child I had an experience of Jesus's love that changed my life. I tell you this story for two reasons. The first is to illustrate the universal nature of the Love on Every Breath meditation and show how a similar spiritual practice, but in a Christian context, spontaneously arose in me as a child. The second is to illustrate the purifying and healing power of this kind of practice. One day when I was seven, I was at my best friend's house, and we were visiting her fifteen-year-old brother in his room. At one point he asked us to pull down our pants, and he briefly put his hand on my vulva. As soon as that happened, I felt uncomfortable. I immediately pulled up my pants and stepped back from him. He didn't pursue it. I fled their house and went home.

From that point on, I felt that something dirty had happened to me. I felt tainted where he had touched me. I felt damaged. Up until then, I had felt a wholesome good feeling inside myself. All of a sudden it wasn't there. I had no idea about sex then, but it just felt bad. And the feeling would not go away. So I decided that I must do something about it. In church I had been taught that God was omnipotent wisdom, love, and compassion, and that Jesus, as the son of God, was God's love for us made manifest. In church I had learned to pray to Jesus both in formal prayers and in my own way. So I decided to call on Jesus to help me.

Every night before I went to sleep, I'd call upon Jesus and imagine that he came to be with me. I would see him up above me, standing next to my bed. He would put his hand, filled with love and compassion, on top of my head. Then a stream of white light would come from his hand into me. The white light filled my body completely and cleaned the bad feeling away. I was being filled with love and healing from Jesus. I did this every night, and it slowly released my feelings of dirtiness and shame.

After about a year, I thought, *I feel completely purified, completely okay, filled with light. I don't need to do this anymore.* I did the meditation one last time, and then with much gratitude, I thanked Jesus for helping me. I never told anyone what had happened.

Many children and adults instinctively want to heal and take away the suffering from themselves and others. I now believe that my intuitive and spontaneous idea to call on Jesus, and to picture his healing light pouring into me, was a natural, self-generated meditation similar to the Love on Every Breath meditation that I offer to you in this book. The feeling of Jesus's healing white light coming into my body from the top of my head is similar to the visualization of Chenrezig,* the Bodhisattva† of Compassion, who sits on a lotus above our head in Love on Every Breath. My experience of

6

---

*   Chenrezig's name in Sanskrit is Avalokitesvara. I have chosen to use the Tibetan version, since this meditation has been primarily practiced in Tibet.

†   A bodhisattva is one who dedicates their life to following the path of awakening in order to free all beings from suffering and to help establish all of us in enlightenment.

feeling sullied, which at the time felt unfortunate, and being cleansed by devotion became a cornerstone of my adult life because it gave me a deep inner knowing. Spiritual practice can work to transform and liberate us.

Love and Compassion

The Dalai Lama has often said, "My religion is kindness." This is not just a simplification for Westerners; in fact, compassion and wisdom form the basis of all Tibetan Buddhism and the essence of all the world's religions. In my opinion, the Dalai Lama is saying that the most important thing for us to have is the actual felt response of a compassionate heart. Loving-kindness and compassion are of utmost importance at this time for humanity. Love and compassion for one another, regardless of race, ethnicity, religion, and gender, need to take precedence over ideology and our superficial differences. We must come together and cooperate with one another in order to survive the global challenges facing us.

From time immemorial there has been, and continues to be, devastating conflict in our world, like wars fought over ethnic, cultural, and religious differences. Power-hungry leaders all over the world use these differences toward divisive ends to inflame hatred and get people to go to war, causing an unfathomable amount of suffering. Buddhism teaches that it is necessary for loving-kindness and compassion for all beings to be in our hearts in order for humanity to move forward in a sustainable way that benefits everyone, leaving no group of people out. Love on Every Breath gives a way to act on this: It frees up our skillful action, so that our efforts in the world are more effective.

The principles of love and compassion form the basis of all religions. In his book *Essential Spirituality*, which describes the seven spiritual practices core to every major religion, Roger Walsh writes, "One emotion has been long praised as supreme by the great religions: love."[1] He goes on to quote *The Encyclopedia of Religions*:

> The idea of love has left a wider and more indelible imprint upon the development of human culture in all its aspects than any other single notion. Indeed, many notable figures…have argued that love is the single most potent force in the universe, a cosmic im-pulse that creates, maintains, directs, informs, and brings to its proper end every living thing.

From a Buddhist point of view, loving-kindness is defined as the sincere wish for the happiness and well-being of others. The next step beyond loving-kindness is compassion. Compassion means feeling someone else's pain or suffering and wishing them to be free of suffering. Of course, this naturally leads to wanting them to be happy. In Mahayana* Buddhism, loving-kindness and compassion are emphasized as essential qualities of who we truly are, qualities we can uncover within ourselves. Buddhism understands that our nature as loving and compassionate people is innate. In a study at the University of British Columbia, researchers found evidence that humans are inherently altruistic. In their study, toddlers under two years of age experienced "greater happiness when giving treats to others rather than receiving treats themselves."[2] Buddha spoke of ignorance as the source of our suffering: ignorance of our

---

* In Sanskrit, Mahayana means "Great Vehicle," and it is one of the three *yanas* or "vehicles" of Buddhism. The Mahayana, the bodhisattva vehicle, is called "great" because its purpose is to liberate all beings.

true nature as well as ignorance of the true nature of all that is. This ignorance brings about habitual patterns of ignorance and suffering that can obscure our inherent altruism. We split reality into self and other, subject and object. It's human nature to seek distinctions. But reality is nondual.* There is no separation between various polarities, but rather truth includes and transcends polarities. Our misunderstanding leads us to desire or grasp for those things and people we want and to have an aversion to and push away those things and people we don't want. This creates habitual patterns: The ego, or our sense of self, devises strategies to try to keep us safe and to get our needs met. But because all phenomena are like a rainbow, what we grasp onto never truly satisfies us.

Therefore, over many centuries, various ways of meditating have been developed to help people uncover and actualize qualities of love in themselves. These meditations spark and develop kindness and compassion in the individual, both for ourselves and for others. This is part of a transformational awakening process for the self — revealing and cultivating the wholesome qualities at the core of who we are. Over time, these kinds of meditations establish us firmly in close contact with our innate love and wisdom while we simultaneously contribute to the larger good. This leads to manifesting compassion in our world. Love on Every Breath is one of these meditations.

Realization

While Love on Every Breath specializes in the cultivation of compassion, it has an aspect of wisdom as well. Buddhism is

---

* Tibetan Buddhism considers reality nondual because it is beyond dualistic conceptions, like self and other, or one and many.

rooted in the fact that liberation is possible for every human being. It is based on the Buddha's own experience of transformation from an ordinary person to a fully free and enlightened being. The Buddha taught a spiritual path that enables people to realize the truth regarding the nature of mind and reality and to arrive at a happiness that is not dependent on outer circumstances.

The essence of Buddhist wisdom is to experience and understand the liberating nature of unconditioned awareness. This awareness is empty in nature. It is not a "thing." It is present but is empty, nonsubstantial. If we look for it, there isn't a thing we can find, but we do find an aware consciousness. Every Tibetan Buddhist meditation begins with letting go of conceptual thought and opening oneself to the truth of what is, right now in our direct experience. This goes beyond the conceptual mind. In other words, we need to let go of thinking and trying to figure everything out. Thinking cannot bring realization. Realization arises out of nonconceptuality. That is why meditation is so important, and why we let go of thinking (again and again for most of us!) during meditation. It is through meditation, a wholesome mind, and wholesome actions that realization occurs. Love on Every Breath is a creative practice (or *kyérim* meditation in Tibetan) that makes use of images and sounds with their symbolic meaning and conscious embodiment of love and compassion.

Complete openness and unbiased awareness are the basis of realization and prepare the practitioner for doing Love on Every Breath. We have to let go — to empty ourselves of concepts — in order to open ourselves to reality. The motivation to meditate is love, which seeks to liberate all beings from suffering, including ourselves. Compassion and love are the intention and aspiration for the meditation practice.

The Eight Steps of Love on Every Breath

The Love on Every Breath meditation has eight steps, which are described in part 2. The complete meditation is done as a sitting practice and takes about forty-five minutes to an hour from start to finish, but the practice is highly adaptable and can be easily abbreviated. I call these abbreviated versions "On-the-Spot" meditations, and I have included them for each step along with the main meditation description. These On-the-Spot variations can be done on their own, individually, anywhere, anytime, in a flash. However, even if you want to practice just one step at a time, I suggest reading through all the steps so that you have a complete understanding of the process. In addition, each step discusses the psychological issues that can arise for meditators during each meditation.

In the book's appendices, I provide the entire Love on Every Breath meditation in both versions — traditional and On-the-Spot — and I also provide a "non-Buddhist" variation for people from other traditions. Each step of the meditation is easily adapted for those of different religions, for those who are nonreligious, and for activists; see "Love on Every Breath for Activists and Those of Other Traditions."

Here is a brief description of each step. In step 1, Resting in Open Awareness, we let go of everything. We let go of the past and the future; we let go of any and all ideas about ourselves or others; we completely let go into our bodies and into relaxing. We become aware of our mind so that we don't allow it to wander into thinking. Rather, we stay present with what is. Usually, the easiest way to do this is to join our attention and breath. This anchors us in our body, and in our felt sensations, instead of in our thoughts. This is a doorway into calm abiding. We simply rest in awareness and openness; openness is synonymous with emptiness.

II

In step 2, Seeking Refuge in Awakened Sanctuary, we go for refuge, for sanctuary, to the awakened ones. This helps create a context and the space for our meditation. We also ask the buddhas and other awakened beings to support us during our meditation.

In step 3, Cultivating Awakened Mind, we engender the altruistic intention to fully awaken to be able to help liberate all beings from suffering.

In the fourth step, Stepping into Love, we invite an awakened being, traditionally Chenrezig (see drawing), the Bodhisattva of Compassion, to be present above the crown of our head.

CHENREZIG, EMBODIMENT OF LOVE

Following our heartfelt prayers, Chenrezig dissolves into ourselves, and we meditate that we become inseparable from Chenrezig. The awakened mind is then established in the heart center as a crystal *vajra* of light (see drawing on facing page), which is a symbol of the indestructible, pure luminous empty reality of who we truly are, our buddha nature. The vajra is what transforms the suffering — not our individual personality or ego. This saves our ego from saying, "I don't want to take in more suffering! I have enough of my own!"

THE VAJRA THAT APPEARS IN OUR HEART CENTER

13

In the fifth step, Taking and Sending for Yourself, we imagine our ordinary self in front of us and contemplate our pain and wounds, meeting ourselves with loving awareness. We breathe in our suffering as a dark smoke-like substance, breathing it right into our heart center. As soon as it touches the vajra of light, we visualize a lightning bolt arising from the vajra, transforming all suffering into white light, symbolic of unconditional awakened love and healing energy. When we are breathing out, this white light goes into the heart center of our ordinary self, where it heals, illuminates, and awakens.

In the sixth step, Taking and Sending for Others, we meditate on a loved one, and gradually we include others. As in the previous step, we contemplate their suffering, big and small, see it as dark smoke, and breathe it into the vajra in our heart. When the suffering touches the vajra, it is instantly transformed. Then, on the out-breath, we imagine the white light going into the person or people, filling them with light and healing, and eventually bringing about their awakening.

Chenrezig, together with the vajra of awakening, greatly enlarges our capacity to welcome the suffering and transform it. Slowly we expand our meditation out to various people and groups of people, until finally all beings are included. We rest in the love and joy of all of us awakened together.

Step 7, Dissolving, involves dissolving our visualization, completely letting go, and resting in open awareness. Then in step 8, Dedicating, we dedicate any and all benefit of our meditation to the awakening of all beings.

Developing Self-Love

14   Traditionally, in Tibet, Love on Every Breath involves first developing compassion and love for ourselves before we do so for others. In the West, many people do not experience self-love, but rather self-criticism and self-hatred. We tend to be overly self-centered and often feel that something is wrong with us. Therefore, it is important that we start the Love on Every Breath meditation by generating compassion and love for ourselves. One of my students, a serious meditator for over thirty years, found that meditating on Love on Every Breath for himself healed a deep psychological angst that had not been touched by many years of quiet sitting meditation. It powerfully liberated wounds he had been carrying for many years.

Without love and compassion for ourselves, we cannot sustain love and compassion for others. Love and compassion can arise spontaneously in certain circumstances for all of us, but to fully *actualize* love and compassion, we need to work through our anger and hurt and have compassion and love for ourselves. Then we can authentically have more compassion for others. Otherwise, it is like living in a home where we behave with harshness and cruelty and then expect to go outside and be open and loving. If we do not include ourselves in our love, our love is not whole, not complete. This is essential. As Aristotle wrote (in *Ethics*, book 9), "All friendly feelings for others are an extension of a man's feelings for himself." It should be noted that self-love and compassion are not to be confused with self-centeredness or narcissism.

Developing love and compassion helps us to grow spiritually and emotionally by lessening our ego fixation and self-centeredness and helping our relationships with others. When we generate compassion, we do not excuse or condone our own or others' negative actions. Likewise, awakened love does not enable our own or others' negativity or destructiveness. Awakened compassion understands that everyone is trying to be happy. We often try to be happy in all the wrong ways, such as when we think that money, prestige, and power will bring us happiness. Some people think they will be happy by stepping on, cheating, or destroying others, but we can have compassion for them in their ignorance. This does not mean we endorse or in any way condone their behavior. We need to stand up to their destructive agendas. Our compassion means that we wish for them to be authentically happy and free of suffering — in other words, awakened.

Four Benefits of the Meditation

I see four major benefits of the Love on Every Breath meditation. First, it can crack open the hard shell of our ego-clinging. Ego-clinging is our grasping onto the self that we think we are, but which isn't actually there. Our sense of self is simply a collection of our perceptions, feelings, thoughts, memories, and consciousness; in part, it arises from the fact that we have a body. Clinging to this separates us from others, puts us first, and blocks our capacity to realize our true nature of wisdom and love. In cracking open our hard shell of self-importance and self-protection, Love on Every Breath allows our natural love and compassion to both be uncovered and grow. It allows our inherent wisdom to shine through. Letting go of ego-clinging is a process that needs to happen again and again. Then we can learn to take loving care of ourselves from a place of increased freedom.

All authentic gurus and teachers give guidance in order for their students to access their own innate wisdom. This is for the sole purpose of helping students awaken. It is not about the teacher. They are not in the business of being an autocrat. Teachers who have the style of a dictator are usually getting their ego's needs met in an unhealthy way by having students idealize them and follow their every command.

Second, Love on Every Breath gives us a process to engage in when we are aware of suffering. It empowers us to transform our experience of the world, of others, and of ourselves. It empowers us to move from feeling overwhelmed or afflicted by suffering to a place of agency. It gives us something to do even when, on an external level, there may be no action to take. In highly developed meditators, and sometimes spontaneously with any of us, the Love on Every Breath meditation can have a significant effect on those people we are sending love to, in terms of alleviating their suffering and shifting their experience to one of being loved. In any case, when we let go of our fixed ideas of other people, the space that is freed up allows for new possibilities to emerge. Our relationships often improve and outcomes are better.

Third, instead of clinging to a fixated ego perspective, we can learn to love ourselves and others more deeply, to have compassion for ourselves and one another. A fresh, open space is created in our mind for the people we know. This shifts our relationships. We stop projecting the past onto others. Then enhanced skillfulness and effectiveness emerge in our words and actions.

Fourth, in shifting away from ego contraction, opening more deeply to love and compassion, and letting go of clinging to our negativity and fear, we can connect with our innate awakened mind, our innate buddha nature (for more, see the next section, "Awakening, Buddha Nature, and Our Subtle Body"). This gives us a deeper sense of our fundamental or basic goodness. This is incredibly healing. We begin to realize that we are not our insecurities, we are not our unwholesome habit patterns, and we are not our neuroses. As we come to more clearly know our natural goodness, we can face and take responsibility for our shadow side, our unconscious material that sometimes acts out or erupts, since we know that is not who we are at our core. Then we can work more consciously and skillfully with our shadow material.

Examples of Compassion: Mark and Linda

An example of this happened in the life of one of my students, Mark, who engaged daily with Love on Every Breath for over a year. Mark was a professor whose department chair, Frank, continually made his life difficult by opposing his ideas and limiting funding opportunities. Mark did not care for Frank at all. However, after practicing Tonglen for many months, Mark decided to focus on this colleague in his meditation. Contemplating Frank's suffering, Mark came to understand

and have compassion for Frank's insecurities and competitiveness. Mark's feelings toward Frank became more neutral; in his mind, there now was a bigger, fresh space for Frank to show up in. The next time they met, Mark engaged Frank with this new attitude. Mark spoke to him without any negative charge, and Frank responded by showing up differently in the relationship. He became much less tense and stopped exhibiting his usual derogatory behavior. Over time, as Mark continued with the meditation, their relationship mellowed and became nonproblematic. Sometimes, when we let go of our end of the rope, the other person does, too.

Another example was Linda, a client who was dying of ALS disease. Once a week, I drove to Linda's home, where she was ensconced in a hospital bed in the living room. Linda was concerned about her six-year-old granddaughter, Laura. Linda's son, Laura's father, was a drug addict, and Laura's mother also had issues that prevented her from being a fit mother. Linda wanted to do something before she died to help her granddaughter.

We decided to work with the Love on Every Breath Tonglen meditation and to focus on an upcoming court hearing that would determine who would take care of Laura. We started the meditation focusing on the child. Over some weeks we expanded our meditation to include the parents, social workers, attorneys, foster parents, and all the other people who were in the child's life and involved in the court case. As the time got closer to the hearing, we imagined the courtroom with all the participants present. We did the meditation for each person involved, including the judge. In Love on Every Breath, you eventually see everyone as healed, illuminated, and awakened. As we did the practice, we saw this happening for everyone. We prayed for the best possible outcome for the child. It was a really tough situation because Laura had no other grandparents, Linda was dying, and there seemed to be no suitable person who could take care of her.

Eventually, the case went to court, and afterward, Linda told me the story, though at this point she could barely speak. An unexpected outcome had occurred. Out of the blue, one of Laura's former foster parents, who was eminently suitable, had come forward. Laura had bonded well with her and her family, but at the time, she had not been able to stay long-term with them. This family only fostered children temporarily who were in crisis. After considering all the evidence, including this previous foster mom's testimony, the judge awarded long-term custody to the previous foster family, who were now able and willing to have Laura. This was indeed a surprising outcome! Linda and I were overjoyed. About ten days later, Linda, now at peace, passed away.

Linda and I had no way of knowing if our meditation helped. But Linda felt really good about what she had been able to do from bed. Who knows what really happened? We were totally okay with not knowing.

Benefits of the On-the-Spot Meditations

Doing the On-the-Spot meditation is valuable in many ways. We can do a step of this transformative meditation anytime. For example, if we hear a parent speaking to their child in an angry voice, or see a news story about refugees fleeing violence, or see an accident on the freeway. This is not a substitute for concrete action in the world, but it does create an internal shift. Opening our heart, we intentionally send out kindness and love.

The "pith essence" or "On-the-Spot" method was taught

to me in my traditional Tibetan training along with the long form. The On-the-Spot method can be used in any moment when you see suffering, whether it is in the grocery store, in traffic, or at a dance concert. I often practice the step Resting in Open Awareness when waiting in line or when enjoying nature. I also attempt to (practice, practice!) let go of my ego's preferences if I am being confronted or am in a challenging conversation. This allows me to relax my defenses and open to what the other person is saying. Then I can hear them, and later I reflect on the value of what they said. We can do this anytime throughout the day to enhance mindfulness and clarity and to let go of unwholesome patterns.

You can start by doing an On-the-Spot meditation two or three times a day, such as at a certain time or during a certain activity. Then you might want to practice doing this many times a day, for example, whenever you stop at a red light, are doing the dishes, or are brushing your teeth. Some people set an alarm on their phone to remind them. We need to make good habits. If we find ourselves in a habitual pattern of irritation, we can remember the possibility that we can drop into resting in awareness for a moment or two. Over time this becomes helpful, as our mind learns how to calm down and relax.

Once we become accustomed to this, we can drop everything and come to a calm state of mind whenever we choose. When we are triggered emotionally, it may be hard to remember, it may take extra time, or it may not be possible at all until the habit of calm abiding is firmly established. "Calm abiding" is one of the translations of the Sanskrit term *samatha*. Another translation is "one-pointed concentration." All meditation done with alertness and mindfulness develops calm abiding. This is good for lowering stress. In challenging situations, this enables us to step back from the emotional charge and allows our wisdom to emerge with greater clarity. Calm abiding can be simultaneous either with witness consciousness or with resting in awareness itself.

The Uniqueness of Love on Every Breath as a Tonglen Meditation

In the standard Tonglen, the meditator simply breathes in the suffering of others and then breathes out love and compassion to them. But this approach does not always work well for Westerners, who often find it difficult to get past the ego's roadblocks. Many people, for example, don't like the idea of taking in someone else's suffering; they say, "I already have enough suffering. I can't handle any more!" Therefore, they turn away from Tonglen, and the opportunity is missed.

Twenty years ago, a highly esteemed Western Buddhist nun, Jetsunma* Tenzin Palmo, was visiting me during her world teaching tour. She was due to teach at a local Zen center one weekend and asked me, "What should I teach?"

"How about Tonglen?" I replied.

"Oh no, people don't like Tonglen. They find it too hard."

"Oh," I said. "I have a special Tonglen from our Shangpa lineage. It changes what is difficult for people and makes it user-friendly!"

She asked me to teach it to her. After learning it, she said to me, "Oh, this is wonderful! May I teach it?"

I attended her teachings that weekend and was glad to see people openly receiving the teaching and not complaining about difficulty with their meditation. I have noticed the

---

* *Jetsunma* is an honorific Tibetan title meaning "venerable" that is bestowed by the head of one's lineage.

same with the many hundreds of people I have taught this meditation to over the years.

It has become clear to me in over forty years of practicing Tonglen, and in thirty years teaching it, that meditating on the embodiment of enlightened love, Chenrezig,* and on the vajra of light, not only increases one's capacity for love but provides a doorway into experiencing one's pure being.

Source of Love on Every Breath Teaching

Many sutras,† commentaries, and meditation practices were brought from India to Tibet between the seventh and thirteenth centuries. Some of these focused primarily on developing and uncovering our innate love and compassion. Love on Every Breath comes from the Shangpa lineage, which, like all authentic Buddhist lineages, traces from disciple to guru, heart student to teacher, back to Buddha Shakyamuni in the fifth century BCE. A guru may have one or two, or occasionally more, heart students who have received and put into practice all their teachings. The gurus are usually accomplished yogis and scholars. As yogis, they are extensively trained in many kinds of meditation and physical yogas. As scholars, they are trained in Dharma and the inner science of the mind, philosophy and logic, medicine, creative arts, and language. The relationship of teacher and student is personal and direct and imbued with great love and mutual respect, though the training and interactions can sometimes

---

* As I mention, you can use a different awakened or divine being if desired; see "Love on Every Breath for Activists and Those of Other Traditions."

† In Sanskrit, *sutra* means a "spiritual discourse," one preserved in the literature of that tradition. In Mahayana Buddhism, it refers to the words of the Buddha and other greatly realized teachers.

take the form of "tough love." In these cases a guru sees what is needed in order for the student to purify themselves and come to full realization.

The Shangpa lineage was started by a Tibetan, Kyungpo Naljor, who reportedly made the trek to India from Tibet seven times to receive teachings and transmissions from the most highly esteemed Buddhist gurus of eleventh- and twelfth-century India. Of these, he said that the kindest and most important to him were two Kashmiri women, Niguma and Sukhasiddhi, each of whom is said to have actualized full and complete awakening. Due to this they are both referred to as "wisdom dakinis." The term *dakini* (or *daka* in the masculine form) covers a wide range.* It means literally "sky dancer." What does this mean? Wisdom dakinis have realized *shunyata,* the open, empty nature of reality, which is sky-like. They play in the sky of shunyata, serving as messengers of awakened compassion and as support for yogis and yoginis (or female yogis). Wisdom dakinis are completely awakened and may teach fortunate disciples. It was not easy for Kyungpo Naljor to become Niguma's student. She rigorously tested him before accepting him. Her tests challenged his concepts about who she was, what he knew, and who he was.

Most of the meditations I practiced in my own three-year retreat were from these two women. It is a great gift that we have these meditations given by two awakened women. The feminine transmission of Niguma and Sukhasiddhi is very simple and direct. Their teachings focus on what is most essential. I received all the transmissions and empowerments of

23

---

*   For more on dakinis, see Judith Simmer-Brown's excellent book, *Dakini's Warm Breath: The Feminine Principle in Tibetan Buddhism.*

the Shangpa lineage from my guru, Kalu Rinpoche,* in 1982. Then the lineage holder, Kalu Rinpoche emphasized the universal nature of compassion meditations, and he was known for teaching many of the great Tibetan masters, as well as being considered a preeminent yogi-scholar and retreat master of the Tibetans in his generation. He also taught many kinds of people all over the globe, including Christian priests and adepts of other religions. He had great confidence in his raggedy band of former hippies, his Western students. I later received these transmissions again from the next primary Shangpa lineage holder, Bokar Rinpoche, in 2001, and again from Tai Situpa in 2009.

In the oral teachings I received from Kalu Rinpoche in his Darjeeling monastery, and in my traditional Tibetan Buddhist three-year retreat of the Shangpa and Kagyu lineages, I was given the extensive teachings that this book offers. Shangpa yogis and yoginis have done this particular meditation for over a thousand years in Tibet. It is a gift to you from the lineage of the eleventh-century enlightened dakinis, Niguma and Sukhasiddhi. It is my wish that through the many people engaging with this meditation, our hearts will open further, and we will bring more love and cooperation into our human world.

Even a Young Child Can Do Love on Every Breath

I have taught an abbreviated version of Love on Every Breath to children. Once I knew a lovely girl named Sarah, then

---

* *Rinpoche* is an honorific title literally meaning "precious one." Either it is given to a person who is found to be an incarnation of an important teacher, or it is given due to a lama's level of activity and realization.

three years old. Sarah was interested in spiritual things and had already learned how to sit quietly for some minutes in meditation. Sarah's godmother brought her to me because Sarah had told her how much seeing certain things upset her. She felt sad when she saw other children hurt or in conflict on the playground. Sarah told me all about this. She was a loving child and was being cared for in a loving way. Sarah also recounted how she often saw dead animals on the road while in the car. This also made her sad. She wanted to know how to help them.

I told her that there was a meditation that can help in these situations. Then I showed her a crystal vajra and told her to imagine a vajra like this, made of light, in her heart. This vajra, I said, was all the Buddha's love and power in her own heart. Then I told her to breathe the person or animal's suffering into the vajra in her heart and imagine that instantly the vajra changed the suffering into healing love and white light. Then she should imagine that this white light was the love and healing energy of the buddhas, and she should send it out into the person or animal. I also taught her that she could do this for herself when she was sad or unhappy. She could breathe her own sadness and unhappiness into the vajra and imagine it instantly changing her feelings into ones of love, peace, and safety.

A few weeks later she came back to see me and happily told me that she really liked doing this practice and it helped her a lot. Sarah, at three years old, was able to do this short meditation practice, giving her something to do in these situations to benefit others and to help herself. This brought her much peace.

The abbreviated form of Love on Every Breath that I taught Sarah is a version of the practice that the Tibetans call the "pith essence," and it's the basis for my "On-the-Spot" meditations. These distill the most important elements of the meditation into its concise version, which can be done anytime, anywhere, by anyone, regardless of religion, age, or educational background. Whether you prefer this distilled form, the traditional form, or to modify the practice to fit your own spiritual path, this book will guide you in developing your own Love on Every Breath meditation.

Love on Every Breath offers a path to feel our innate love and wisdom and to bring these forward into our consciousness and interactions in daily life. Like all Buddhist meditations, it also helps us to realize reality as it is, known in Sanskrit as *dharmata*. This is the basis in Buddhism for the unfolding of wisdom.

Awakening, Buddha Nature, and Our Subtle Body

Your own mind, uncontrived, is the body of
ultimate enlightenment. To remain undistracted
within this is meditation's essential point.
Realize the great, boundless, expansive state.

— NIGUMA, FOREMOTHER OF THE SHANGPA LINEAGE,

FROM HER SONG OF REALIZATION

Suzuki Roshi, the preeminent twentieth-century Zen master who helped establish Zen in America, once said, "Realizing emptiness is like drinking milk at the mother's breast." This means that resting in emptiness nourishes and sustains us. It enables us to grow. A mother nursing her baby is an image of profound connection. This counteracts the notion that realizing emptiness brings us to a disengaged, uncaring attitude, as if emptiness means, "It's all empty, so nothing matters." The vast open expanse, inseparable from awareness itself, is called Prajnaparamita, the Great Mother.

One of my other teachers, Kalu Rinpoche's close beloved disciple, Bokar Rinpoche, once said to us, "There is the nothing-to-do and the must-to-do." That is, there is nothing to do because we are already awakened, but what we must do is discover and realize this for ourselves; otherwise we remain caught in our habitual patterns of ignorance and suffering, failing to reach our full potential.

This section goes in depth into Buddhist teachings in order to set the stage for the Love on Every Breath meditation.

Philosophical Underpinnings

The Love on Every Breath meditation helps us to connect with our awakened nature of wisdom and love. It helps us live moment to moment from our inherent kindness and goodness. It helps us unlock the unlimited wisdom and love at the core of who we are.

Understanding the philosophical underpinnings of Buddhist meditation in general, and Vajrayana meditation in particular, fundamentally supports this process and enhances the power of our meditation to benefit ourselves and others. Buddhism at its core seeks to alleviate suffering. This is what motivated the Buddha to teach and what the entire path of Buddhist practice is designed to liberate us from. The word *dharma* in this context means "the teachings of the Buddha." Dharma helps to alleviate the root of our suffering. Buddha taught that life is characterized by suffering, and the reason we suffer is because we are ignorant of the nature of reality and of who we truly are. In Buddhism, to awaken means that we penetrate the veil of ignorance to realize the true nature or truth of our mind and reality. All Buddhist meditations are designed to assist us to awaken. The Buddha taught that we inherently have the seed potential of enlightenment and, in fact, are already awakened. In a Buddhist context, the English words *awakened* and *enlightened* mean the same thing and are used interchangeably. I usually use the word *awakened* because it implies a process, and awakening is a process.

In order to better understand the Love on Every Breath meditation, we will go over apparent truth and genuine truth, as well as "true nature" and "buddha nature," and how this relates to what is called the "subtle body" and the breath in Vajrayana Buddhism.

It is helpful to look at the larger context of the Vajrayana. Vajrayana is a part of the Mahayana. The Sanskrit term *Mahayana*, or "Great Vehicle," is called the Buddhist vehicle of the bodhisattva path. *Yana* means vehicle in the sense that it takes us to the other shore. This is a famous Buddhist metaphor for awakening from *samsara*, the cyclic existence of suffering, to the freedom and peace of nirvana. The Mahayana encompasses the meditations and their foundations, the philosophical teachings. Together these enable us to achieve the goal of the bodhisattva ideal and path — complete awakening to liberate ourselves and all sentient beings from suffering.

Buddhism teaches that what we usually think of as reality is in fact an illusion. It's not that things and beings don't exist at all — they just don't exist the way we usually think they do. It is an illusion that we are separate beings. The Mahayana standpoint is to fully embrace the illusion with love and caring. Our suffering hurts! Other people's suffering hurts! We deeply feel pain, joy, and the myriad of human emotions. Our path is simultaneously one of realization and love. What we do makes all the difference in the world. Each moment we are experiencing past karma and creating new karma. When we are triggered emotionally, we can stop for a moment before reacting and consciously respond to what is arising. We create our state of mind. If we rest in loving-kindness with others and ourselves, this then is the consciousness we live in.

The Two Truths

Every school of Buddhism has philosophical teachings that form the basis for the various meditations. One of the most important philosophical tenets is called the two truths, which refers to the nature of reality. These two truths are genuine truth and apparent truth, which are also translated as ultimate truth and relative truth. It is very useful on the path of awakening to discuss the two truths. I will do so from a Vajrayana perspective, the larger context of this meditation.

The Buddha taught that genuine truth is beyond the dualisms of apparent truth, beyond the polarities of nonexistence and existence, of nihilism and eternalism. This truth is what Buddha called the "middle way." Further, the phenomena of sights, sounds, sensations, feelings, thoughts, and emotions that we constantly experience are ever-changing, insubstantial, and conceptually designated. All that appears to our senses and our mental faculty arises due to causes and conditions. Apparent truth is the truth of causality: Everything is interdependent. Appearances are not only ever-changing, but the causes and conditions that produce them are empty of true existence. They appear to exist. In actuality they don't exist the way we think they do. But neither are they nonexistent. We live our lives in the apparent truth. The mystery of reality is beyond duality of existence and nonexistence, of subject and object, of one and many.

Realizing the nature of mind and phenomena is the crux of realization in Buddhism. The Buddha taught that the fundamental cause of our suffering is that we think we are individuals. We take the fact that we have a body, perceptions, feelings, thoughts, and consciousness as evidence that we are a self, separate from all else. Everything else becomes "other," and duality is created. Our dualistic worldview is created by this split of subject and object. As the subject, we want to acquire the objects we see as beneficial to us, and we want to get rid of that which we deem unhelpful. We are indifferent to other phenomena that we consider unimportant. As we grasp at objects that do not truly exist (they are not separate, solid, or permanent), we are frustrated and dissatisfied with the results of this process. True satisfaction and happiness come from realizing the genuine truth beyond this apparent reality.

Genuine truth is the unchanging, nondual, irreducible nature of mind and reality. It is pure, uncontrived, unimpeded awareness. All that is, all phenomena, has the same true nature and manifests inseparably as the union of form and emptiness. The two truths are inseparable. The true nature of apparent reality is genuine reality.

It is said that the Buddha realized the genuine truth of all that is, and he fully understood apparent reality and how it functions. He could see all the causes and effects playing out. He sometimes talked about what he saw and knew on the apparent level, for example, explaining to people what they had done in a past life. On the Buddhist path we train in realizing and resting in the simultaneity of genuine and apparent reality. Nevertheless, it is realization of the genuine truth that sets us free.

When we realize genuine reality, love arises as a response of our true heart to ourselves and others. In the words of the third Karmapa,* Rangjung Dorje (1284–1339 CE), in the Aspiration of Mahamudra Prayer:

> *While the nature of beings has always been full*
>   *enlightenment,*
> *Not realizing this, they wander in endless samsara.*
> *For the boundless suffering of sentient beings*
> *May overwhelming compassion be born in my being.*
>
> *While such compassion is active and never ending,*
> *In the moment of compassion, its essential nature is*
>   *nakedly clear.*†
> *This conjunction is the undeviating supreme path;*
> *Inseparable from it, may I practice it day and night.*³

This quote from one of the most beloved prayers of the Tibetans acknowledges the genuine reality that beings are awakened but do not know it. The Karmapa prays for monumental compassion to be born in himself to address the apparent truth of the suffering of beings. In the midst of vast compassion, the experience of the emptiness of self, the emptiness of the activity (compassion), and the emptiness of the one receiving the compassion, the 24/7 meditation is resting in the union of these two truths. Love meets the insubstantial, rainbow-like suffering of beings, soothing the pain. Resting uninterruptedly in the two truths is called stabilization. Generally, this is quite a process, as we get thrown out of our realization by the strength of our habitual patterns and back into duality as soon as we get triggered mentally or emotionally.

32

---

* Karmapa is the head of the Kagyu lineage. Currently, the seventeenth incarnation, Ogyen Trinley Dorje, is based in India, having escaped the Chinese government in Tibet when he walked over the Himalayas at age fifteen.

† That is, "its essential nature" is shunyata, or emptiness.

Resting in true nature and meeting our experience with love purifies and liberates our karma, and it brings all our qualities into full manifestation.

What is our true nature? What is the genuine truth? These are not seen as two separate things in Buddhism. The genuine truth is that everything seems to exist but is empty of actually existing. Phenomena like trees, mountains, rivers, animals, humans, buildings, and cars appear to exist but do not. In an apparent sense they do, of course. True nature is that phenomena and emptiness are connate, inseparable. Genuine reality is referred to as appearance-emptiness, awareness-emptiness.

The vast empty nature of everything is called shunyata. It is the union of form and emptiness. In the Heart Sutra, the most famous Mahayana scripture, Chenrezig states:

33

Form is empty, emptiness is form. Emptiness is not other than form; form is not other than emptiness. In the same way, feeling, discrimination, formation, and consciousness are empty.

Thus, Shariputra, all phenomena are emptiness: They have no characteristics, no birth, no cessation, no stains, no freedom from stains, no decrease, and no increase.

Thus, Shariputra, in emptiness there is no form, no feeling, no discrimination, no formation, no consciousness; no eye, no ear, no nose, no tongue, no body, no mind; no form, no sound, no smell, no taste, no tactile sensation, no phenomenon; no eye-faculty potential, no mental-faculty potential, no mental-consciousness potential, and nothing in between; no ignorance nor any ending of ignorance, no aging and death nor any ending of aging and death, and nothing in between.[4]

Genuine reality is not simply emptiness. Awareness itself is empty, yet present. All that is, is the union of awareness and emptiness. However, we have split reality into a dualistic experience. Awareness is said to be luminous clarity. The most profound realization in Tibetan Buddhist teachings is called "realizing the true nature of mind." In this usage, mind means awareness or consciousness. There isn't a reality outside of mind. Everything is inseparable from mind, from awareness or consciousness. This does not fit into our concepts of what is true at all. It doesn't seem logical to us. This is why it is said that reality as it is (*dharmata* in Sanskrit) is beyond concept. It is not possible to have realization of true nature through the thinking mind. The thinking mind operates in a dualistic way. Thinking is basically a binary process where truth is either this or that. But genuine truth is beyond polarity. Realization of genuine truth happens in direct experience. We need to have stable concentration, called *samatha* in Sanskrit, and then direct our concentration to investigate the nature of reality in our direct experience. This is called *vipashyana** in Sanskrit, meaning "insight" or "inquiry."

Kalu Rinpoche illustrated our own inner awakened nature to us once by holding up a large, pristine crystal and covering it up with many layers of his robe. He explained that the robe symbolizes the many layers of ignorance that hide the beautiful awake radiance of who we truly are. The path in Buddhism is peeling off the layers. Meditation, study, and living with kindness and integrity allow us to move past the obscurations blocking us from reaching awakening.

---

* Readers may be more familiar with the Pali spelling *vipassana*.

Who we truly are is luminosity, clarity, and emptiness. Who we truly are is the inseparable union of wisdom and love. Who we truly are is radiant goodness. This is our buddha nature, which is a seed, our potential for enlightenment. However, buddha nature is not a thing — if we look for it, we won't see it. This is called "being empty of being a thing." We know that our mind is not a thing. But we think that our mind is dependent on our brain, encapsulated in our body. This is not the case. Who we truly are is deathless and birthless. Consciousness can and is obscured on an apparent level, but not in actuality. It is primordially pure.

From the perspective of genuine reality, we are already awakened. The difficulty is that we do not realize who and what we are. One of the Sanskrit terms for our innate awakened nature is *tathagatagarbha*. *Tathagata* means "thus gone one," gone beyond *samsara*. This refers to all the buddhas, the fully enlightened ones. *Garbha* means "potential" or "seed." *Buddha* means "awakened" or "enlightened." Our buddha nature is the seed potential we all have for full enlightenment. The seed will grow into a vibrant, alive plant if given the right conditions. Not only that, it is the part of us that is always awake. That has always been awake. We are usually completely out of touch with this aspect of ourselves. Of course, in actuality, our buddha nature pervades ourselves as well as all that is, but from a relative point of view, we can speak of it as a part of ourselves.

There is a famous metaphor for our buddha nature. We are walking along a dusty road and feel something in the dust under our feet. We reach to pick it up, clean it off, and it turns out to be a jewel! Do we keep it with us, or do we throw it back onto the ground? This is our situation. There is a jewel, our buddha nature, inside of us, covered over. Are we going to pick it up and cherish it or ignore it, leaving it on the road in the dust?

Jennifer Welwood captures this in her poem "The Jewel Inside":

The jewel inside has grown dusty.
What out there could have captured you so
That you forgot all about this one?
Feel the tragedy of that error.
And see: Even now, the tears of your grief
Are washing the dust away.[5]

Our Awakened Nature and Our Shadow Side

The Love on Every Breath meditation helps us to connect with our awakened nature. We become aware of this by noticing in the moment, and in later reflection, those instances where our spontaneous goodness emerged, the times when our hearts were moved and we simply acted. For example, people who leap to help another in distress, even at the risk of their own safety. We all have the inherent tendency to come to the aid of someone in distress. We can also see in ourselves the kernel of goodness that underlies what we do. For example, the teenager who wants to go to college to become a teacher, so she can help inner-city kids learn and grow, or the man who shields another with his body. For some of us, the layers covering our altruism are many, but nevertheless it is there in all of us. As we become aware of this basic goodness in ourselves, it gives us a glimpse of our awakened nature. We begin to have a felt sense of our inherent goodness and loving-kindness. It's like the sun poking its head out from behind the clouds. It is helpful if we acknowledge this in ourselves and in other people. We can learn to rest in this more and more and cultivate the closeness with our essence.

If we usually don't see our true nature, we also don't see our shadow side. Both of these are incredibly important, as getting in touch with our basic goodness not only is the path to realization but helps us face our shadow. Connecting with our basic goodness is not about feeding the ego. It's not narcissistic and doesn't increase our narcissism. It joins us with our humility and compassion. The more we can feel our true goodness, the more we are able to look at, be with, and work through our shadow material. Once we know that our neurotic, confused, insecure, aggressive parts are not who we are, it gives us courage to consciously work with our shadow side. Otherwise, it is too scary. If we don't have enough sense of our basic goodness, the ego will block us from looking at our more neurotic parts because it can't handle it. It's too disconcerting. It feels dangerous to the ego.

We defend against seeing our negativity, our control issues, and our ego strategies. We can't bear to face them because we think that is who we are. When we know that is not who we are, we become willing and courageous enough to face ourselves. We can transform. We can allow our negative patterns to be liberated by not acting them out. For most of us, this is a long-term project. It doesn't happen overnight. We have to quiet the voice inside that tells us we are not up to the task. But what is the other option? Not waking up? Life will provide us with suffering either way. Then our happiness is always transitory, dependent on good circumstances. And good circumstances are not always under our control. This is an opportunity to turn our suffering into the path of awakening.

Subtle Body Teachings

The subtle body is not physical reality but rather a pattern in the interface between mind and body. It is the intersection of our material and nonmaterial manifestation. It is a phenomenon and, as such, is an apparent truth, just like our physical body. On the path of awakening it is purified, transformed, developed, and eventually awakened. Awakening is not only mental. It happens in the entirety of who we are, including in the physical and subtle bodies.

Centuries of meditation and yogic practice have brought understanding about the subtle body, which comprises what are called in Sanskrit *nadis* (channels, pronounced "nadees"), *prana* (movement, air principle, closely connected with the breath), and *bindu* (energetic aliveness or vital energy in every molecule). In Tibetan these are called *tsa, lung,* and *tigli.* The chakras are energetic centers within the central channel.* In Love on Every Breath, we work with and in the heart chakra. The central channel is said to be about a dime's width, and it runs from the root chakra in the genital area straight up to the crown chakra at the top of the head, slightly in front of the spine. The prana runs through the central channel as well as through the other eighty-four thousand channels said to be in the subtle body. For unawakened beings, the prana is restricted, running through the channels that are wired according to our neurotic habit patterns and karma. The suboptimal wiring of the channels creates blocks and detours in the flow of prana, causing the prana to flow in less-than-advantageous ways. It is said that after enlightenment, the *nadis* in the Buddha's subtle body were completely rewired in the optimal way. Researchers who investigate the

38

---

* The central channel is called in Sanskrit the *sushumna* or *avadhuti*, and in Tibetan the *tsa uma.*

relationship between meditation and the brain are finding that this rewiring is not metaphorical, but actual.[6]

The Importance of Posture and Eye Placement

Posture is critical for meditation and for rewiring to occur. There are various points of posture, but the first step, and most crucial, is to sit upright. This allows the subtle body channels to straighten and the prana to flow in a proper way. It allows for natural presence to open and stabilize. You want to be comfortable without tension. If normally you do not have great posture, sitting up straight may be uncomfortable at first and take a while to get used to. It is good to have someone well versed in meditation posture check you out. Oftentimes, we can't tell for ourselves if we are leaning to the front or back or to one side. It is optimal to sit cross-legged but it is not necessary. Masters agree that sitting in a chair is fine, as long as the posture is correct. You may need a pillow under your bum to ensure that you are not leaning back. Many chairs are angled the exact wrong way for good posture. Once you are seated properly, relax into your body, maintaining your healthy posture. Again, relaxing may take a bit of time, but if you stay with good posture and consciously let go of tension, it will become comfortable.

As for eye placement, in Vajrayana Buddhism, we meditate with eyes open. An exception to this is when you are doing a meditation involving lots of imagination or visualization; then it is okay to close your eyes. When your eyes are open, let go of the tendency to grab on to the visual field. This is an unconscious tendency — we can become aware of this and let it go. Instead, let your gaze be soft, and let your eyes look slightly downward, at a forty-five-degree angle. Let your eye consciousness be open, without grabbing on to anything visually. Don't block your field of vision either. For Love on Every Breath, have your eyes open for the first and last step of resting in awareness. In the creative phase of the meditation, when you are visualizing, it is fine to close your eyes to aid concentration.

Eventually, keeping the eyes open during the creative phase is valuable in order to be able to rest in awareness during our moment-to-moment daily experience. In this way we can mix meditation with daily life. This also helps with realization of our true nature. If all our senses are open, without any grabbing on or pushing away, we can rest in the vividness of our present experience. Eventually, we can come to realize the essential, unchanging, and self-liberating essence of all our experience. In our Mahamudra tradition, specific instructions and inquiries done in meditation help bring this to fruition.

Activities like yoga, meditation, qigong, and tai chi can rewire our subtle body. The channels open and straighten, allowing prana to circulate more evenly and fully. However, our mind also needs to change; we need to work on disengaging from and releasing unwholesome habit patterns, or the rewiring won't stick. You may have noticed this if you have done a lot of yoga — you can feel incredibly good after a yoga session, until your normal neurotic patterns rear their head, and if you act them out, they may affect the body. For example, when I was doing hours a day of hatha yoga in my early twenties, sometimes I would feel so light that I would eat too much after yoga. It felt like I was taking two steps forward, one step backward.

Watching the breath also helps bring the mind to peace. Every time we relax and become present in our basic meditation practice, our prana settles down because mind and prana are strongly linked. This is one of the reasons that meditation de-stresses us. The subtle movement of prana in the body and the mind intimately affect each other. If the mind is agitated, there is corresponding agitation in the subtle body, affecting the physical body. This happens with emotions as well. An easy way to understand this is in the experience of anxiety or fear. When we are anxious, we may feel butterflies in our stomach or our heart may be racing. If we are suddenly afraid, we may get the feeling that our heart is in our throat. The latter is the prana rising up the central or side channels too quickly. Tibetan Buddhist yogic literature states, "Where mind goes, prana goes; where prana goes, mind goes." When we actively engage with our breath with specific breathing practices, called grabbing hold of prana, both the mind and the movement of energy in the body can be directed toward awakening, toward the cultivation of love and other qualities.

41

Love on Every Breath works with the breath as well as with our spiritual, mental, emotional, physical, and subtle body aspects all at once to hasten awakening. The breath is used as a tool for awakening our love and heart chakra. This is different from the way most meditators watch or follow the breath, as a way of stabilizing the mind in concentration. In this meditation, one directs the breath in and out of the heart center, bringing the mind and awareness into the heart center. The breath is employed as part of an internal transformational process.

A Subtle Body Experience

Transmission of awakened mind from a teacher to a student, through touch or mind-to-mind connection, can be powerful. For a student, it can be simply an "aha moment," an energetic opening experience, or it can occur in other ways. I had a subtle body energetic experience of this in my late twenties while in the Himalayan foothills. The sixteenth Karmapa had his main monastery outside Tibet in Sikkim, a country annexed in the midseventies by India. In those days we needed a special permit to go to Sikkim, due to border issues between India and China. These permits were quite complicated to obtain, but I managed to get one in Darjeeling. I made my way, with a friend, to Gangtok, the capital of Sikkim, and the next day, in an old English jeep from the 1940s, piled high with huge sacks of cilantro and filled with people. It was 1978, and in those days, the only cars available were old jeeps that the British had left behind when they gave India its independence in 1947. We climbed into one, and off we drove to His Holiness Karmapa's monastery. We jolted along the curvy mountain road for about an hour, until we arrived at the gates of the temple compound.

That first trip I stayed just four days. An extraordinary thing happened on the last day. My friend had already departed, so I went to say good-bye to Karmapa on my own. When greeting or taking leave of a high lama, it's traditional to offer a *kata*, a white silk scarf, which is symbolic of offering our pure heart. Early morning, *kata* in hand, I went to see His Holiness to give him my deep gratitude and to say good-bye. He was in his private home on the monastery grounds, sitting in a room with many windows looking out onto the evergreens and snowcapped mountains.

As I sat in front of Karmapa on the floor, he reached out and put his hand, palm down, on top of my head, on my crown chakra. Then he started chanting and chanting. I couldn't believe it; it seemed like twenty minutes. Energy poured into my crown chakra and down what I later learned was my central channel (I knew nothing about this at the time). I was shy at that age and thought, *Oh my gosh.* My central channel, the whole inside core of my body, became large, completely empty, and filled with his blessing. My central channel opened up to include the whole world. It was a powerful experience, the feeling of openness and inseparability with the whole planet and beyond. My subtle body was never the same after that.

Meditating on specific chakras or on the channels of the subtle body have different effects, depending on the meditation. Himalayan people feel that their mind is in their heart chakra. Richard Davidson, a researcher at the University of Wisconsin, who has worked with the Dalai Lama and advanced Buddhist yogis, once recounted a funny moment. He had hooked a few monks up with wires all over their heads, as part of his research on whether meditating on compassion and loving-kindness affects the brain. The monks started laughing uncontrollably. Finally, Davidson asked them, "What's so funny?" They replied, "You want to research love and compassion, but you hooked up our heads, not our hearts!" It is interesting that, in the West, we feel that our mind is in our head. I met one Tibetan who at age seventeen had been recognized as a reincarnated lama by the Dalai Lama. This man confided in me that he had been educated in Western-type schools in India and had always felt that his mind was in his head. He told me, "I had to train my mind to stay in my heart!"

Meditating in the Heart Chakra

Loving-kindness practices focus on the heart chakra, as this has been considered the home of the mind, where both love and wisdom have their seat.

In Love on Every Breath, we breathe into and out from the heart chakra. This is similar to an experience during a physical therapy session, when the therapist might say, "Breathe into your lower back." You bring your attention into the tight spot and breathe into it. The actual breath doesn't go there, but it feels like it does. What goes there is our prana.

When we breathe into our heart chakra, the prana is brought there. Awareness and breath together are very powerful healing and transformational tools. In this meditation, transformation takes place in the heart chakra, and this affects the whole of us. Over time, and sometimes in powerful experiences, our heart chakra opens more. Conscious engagement with the breath has different benefits, depending on the specific breath practice. Working with the mind and breath simultaneously helps to transform neurotic habit patterns into wisdom and awakening.

Dharma practice, certain kinds of exercise, and spiritual transmission can rewire our mind-body system. We need to be open in order for this to happen. The innate wisdom of the body asserts itself when we get out of the way. This body wisdom seeks to unblock our channels, allowing prana to flow fully through. When we meditate in specific ways on the circulation of prana through channels and in chakras, it purifies our mind and karma and detoxes the body. It readies the subtle system for awakening to occur.

As I mention above, specific kinds of movement, like yoga, especially when coupled with the breath, are designed to benefit the subtle body. Exercise in general, such as walking, running, and swimming, is good for the subtle body as well.

In long Vajrayana meditation training retreats, there are strong, vigorous series of physical yogas that we engage in, in addition to the meditation training done in sitting posture. These yogas, called *trulkor* in Tibetan, powerfully renovate the subtle body to hasten the awakening process. There are particular correlations with the subtle body and various meditative experiences as well as with stages of realization. After engaging intensively in these kinds of spiritual practices for years, I went through a spontaneous process that felt as if I was being rewired. I thought this was completely metaphorical, and only in the subtle body, until some years later, when research began to come out that the rewiring can be traced in the brain. Not surprisingly, when our subtle body feels good, so do we, and vice versa.

Love on Every Breath engages our subtle body, working specifically with the heart chakra, light and form, sound (when doing the mantra), and the breath. The subtle body can develop so that it supports us in awakening. Awakening is both a mental and physical experience, so if we work with both of these simultaneously, it hastens the full blossoming of our wisdom and love.

Part Two

THE MEDITATION

Love on Every Breath
in Eight Steps

Resting in Open Awareness

You do not need to know what is happening,
or where it is all going. What you need to recognize are
the possibilities and challenges offered by the present moment,
and to embrace them with courage, faith, and hope.
The world is transparent and the divine is shining
through all the time.

— THOMAS MERTON

*I*n the late seventies and early eighties, I spent some years in the eastern Himalayas, primarily in Bhutan, where I lived, and in Darjeeling and Sikkim. I often stayed in Rumtek in Sikkim for a month or more in order to be with His Holiness the sixteenth Karmapa. Since his first incarnation, Karmapa has consciously chosen to take birth again and again as a human being in order to be of benefit, and his immense wisdom and love is legendary among the Tibetans, Sikkimese, and Bhutanese. He started the *tulku* reincarnation system among the Tibetans. He is the only *tulku*, or reincarnated lama, of the Tibetans who leaves a letter telling where he will be reborn in his next life. He, like the Dalai Lama, is considered to be an emanation of the Bodhisattva of Compassion. After awakened beings leave their body, they are beyond limitations, established in ultimate freedom. Time and space do not hinder them. Their spontaneous, awakened, compassionate activity emanates into various worlds. On our planet, these emanations are usually human. The Karmapa is one such remarkable being. There is no need to believe this or not. It doesn't matter one way or another. What matters is that someone like the Karmapa has the aspiration and capacity to inspire many people to develop spiritually and to live with an open heart.

The sixteenth Karmapa was exceedingly kind to me, as he was with everyone who came to see him, rich or poor, interested in Dharma or not. I could visit him whenever I liked. In addition to his house on the grounds of the monastery, he also had rooms above the main *lhakhang*, or temple. He could often be found there in his large reception room. There was usually a translator with him and an attendant or two in rooms nearby. Over and over, I had a striking experience with His Holiness: Every time I walked into his room, His Holiness's vast, open presence became palpable, and my mind would become like a huge blank movie screen. Whatever thought was in my mind, such as what I was going to speak with His Holiness about, I would immediately recognize as insignificant ego activity, and I would drop it. I would just be totally open and present with him the rest of the time. It was a powerful introduction to resting in awareness.

The First Step in Meditation

When you have no clinging to what appears, what arises,
It frees itself within its own ground.

— NIGUMA, SONG OF REALIZATION

In general, the first step in meditation is to focus on posture. Align your body so that your back is upright, and you are not leaning to the left or right, forward or backward. Your chin should be slightly tucked downward, so that your eyes are naturally at a forty-five-degree angle. For this part of the meditation, leave your eyes open, with a soft gaze. Notice if your eyes grab on to sights. Eye consciousness includes the sights and your eyes. Draw this consciousness back into your eyes, and then let it relax in its place, open, not grasping at the sights, and not pushing them away either. Thoughts will ususally continue to arise, but simply let go of them.

Start fresh again and again, letting go into openness, letting go of concepts, and letting go into what is, right now, here, in the moment. Relax into your body and feel the sensations. The difference between a meditation of resting in awareness and simply spacing out is that your mind settles as you let go of thoughts. Your usual frame of reference shifts and opens, and you come into the present moment, resting in the open, vivid clarity of mind and experience.

Begin this meditation by focusing on your breath. Feel the breath moving in and out of your body. A nice way to start is to breathe kindness into your heart chakra, and relax as you breathe out. Meditate like this until it feels stable. Allow your awareness to radiate out and gradually encompass your entire body. Stay in touch with your breath. When awareness feels stable, let go of a sense of the boundaries of your body, while still staying in touch with your sensations, and let your mind open to the greater space. Rest in awareness and allow your mind to be like the sky — open, unimpeded, unbound. This is an opportunity to let go of life's demands, thoughts, and concerns. Let go of thoughts of the past, of the future, and of critiquing what is happening in present time. Clear your mind of preferences and judgments that inhibit objective clarity. Open to the vividness of the immediate experience of your body and all that is. Let go into your felt experience, just as it is, right in this moment. Let everything be, both in your inner and outer experience. This allows the natural unfolding of insight and wisdom to occur.

Opening to our felt experience and into the larger space helps our subtle body channels to open. If we breathe consciously into the body while simultaneously relaxing, the prana will circulate in healing ways. The channels that are open receive more prana. This heals and invigorates us. Relaxing into our breath allows the natural openness and clarity to flow, relax, clean out our *nadis*, release old patterns, and open up subtle-body pathways.

As our meditation continues, we have to let go of thoughts again and again. Shifting away from thinking is a meditative training process that becomes easier and easier as we build up the tools of the witness — mindfulness and alertness. These allow us to notice what our mind is doing in any instant. We can choose then to let go of thoughts instead of continuing down that road. Thoughts will continue to arise. This is normal, as our habitual patterns are persistent. It's like diverting a stream that has been flowing in a particular direction for a long time. It takes a redirecting of our attention and focus by simply noticing that we are thinking and then dropping the thoughts, returning to rest our mind in awareness. We gradually build our capacity to focus and stay with the particular meditation. We learn to be fully present in this moment, and the next, and the next.

Connecting with our felt sense of the body helps to stabilize our minds. If we join our mind with our breath, this helps to anchor us in our body. Joining attention and the breath is slightly different than watching the breath. The joining collapses any space between the breath and the watcher. This collapses the dualities of the watcher and the breath, the watcher and the body, thereby moving toward healing our split between subject and object. Joining with the sensations of the body, we allow our whole body to be present in our awareness.

The Dance of Form and Formlessness

Love on Every Breath begins and ends with resting in open awareness in formless meditation. After the beginning, it then moves to a creative meditation process — a meditation with form, which utilizes visualization, breath, prayer, and mantra as the meditation unfolds. The dance of formlessness and form — the two inseparable truths of genuine and apparent reality — moves together. Meditating on formlessness and form is a process used in Vajrayana meditation that helps transform and liberate our persistent patterns and conditioning, bringing us closer to the truth of who we are, and bringing us to realization of the nonduality of form and emptiness. For example, when we are engaging in a meditation with form, like when praying or saying mantras, we practice simultaneously resting in formlessness. There are many aspects of nonduality to realize: movement and stillness, mind and heart, subject and object (or self and other), phenomena and emptiness, the experiencer and the experience, awareness and phenomena, the true nature of ourselves and all that is, love and emptiness, compassion and emptiness, awareness and emptiness. Once we realize true nature, all dualities are seen through and drop away.

In order for realization to occur, the ego needs to let go, again and again, into the greater reality. By greater reality, I mean the truth that is bigger than we are, bigger than our world as we usually know it. In Buddhism, philosophers articulate this as the true, unchanging nature of all that is. This truth reveals itself to us in our experience. It is incomprehensible to our intellectual understanding until it is fully realized. To understand truth requires the insight that arises when our mind is concentrated, stabilized, and able to explore with awareness, rather than with thinking, what our experience is in the moment.

Our spiritual practice and daily experience work to soften clinging to our ego's strategies. They prod, push, and sometimes corner our ego in order to open up space for new experience and new growth. If we continue to tightly adhere to our ego's viewpoint and strategies, as is natural, realization cannot occur. The silver lining of challenging circumstances is that our old strategies may not work anymore, and we have to let go of them to see what might work. This is where the application of Dharma can greatly transform us.

Living in the Himalayas, I was fortunate to spend time with female practitioners — yoginis, or *naljorma*, as they are called in Tibetan. They rarely spoke. But watching them, feeling their presence, was a nonverbal transmission — how they conducted themselves, how they integrated their meditation into every movement. Every moment with them brought me to settle in contentment and peace.

Witness Consciousness

That which we witness, we are forever changed by,
and once witnessed we can never go back.

— ANGELES ARRIEN

Usually when we are thinking or ruminating, we identify with the active part of consciousness. We miss that there is an awake, ever-present awareness behind the thoughts. The way to let go of thoughts is to develop witness consciousness. Witness consciousness is that part of our mind that notices what is going on, both with ourselves and in our world. When we rest in witness consciousness, we notice the thoughts going through our mind. In meditation, we let go of all our thoughts of the past — for example, of what we ought to have done, what could have been, what others have done, and what has happened. Then we let go of thinking about the future — what we could do, what might happen, what we'd like to happen. Then we let go of evaluating and critiquing the present — what we like or don't like in this moment and our judgments of ourselves and others. Thinking about the past and the future and evaluating the present keep us out of the moment. These thoughts keep us in our heads in fantasy, judgment, preferences, and prejudices, which all obscure the natural clarity of our mind.

When we have stabilized the witness consciousness, it grows in strength in our everyday life. We begin to recognize more and more what is going on in our mind. This allows us to steer clear of the "bad neighborhoods" of our mental processes. For example, we can catch that we are once again going down the road of berating ourselves, and we can choose to let go. Or as the great Dzogchen master Dudjom Rinpoche once said to my friend, "Just change the channel."

55

But even more importantly, because it affects us more in the long run, witness consciousness allows us to discern when the voice of our ego consciousness speaks in our mind, or if someone else's ego voice resounds in our mind, like old messages we heard in childhood from a parent. Then we can notice the consciousness that is aware of this. This consciousness is much more objective in the sense of not having preferences. It has balance as it perceives, it does not have emotional reactivity, and it is kind. This is our awake, ever-present awareness showing through. Over time it becomes easier to see what is going on in our mind. We can allow our voice of wisdom to come through. Realization and actualization of our true nature does not happen when we are in ego consciousness, our usual state of consciousness. In the way described above, meditation helps us to first distinguish ego consciousness from the witness, and then from awareness itself. This is not a one-time process. Once we learn how to do it, as we notice what is happening in our minds in meditation and daily life, we shift again and again from ego consciousness to witnessing, and eventually to awareness itself.

After witness consciousness has been firmly established, we can see through the illusion of "the one who witnesses." At some point we realize that there is no actual witness. The witness is "empty" of true existence. There is no one there, and nevertheless, there is awareness that has no reference point. Witness consciousness gives way to our awake, true nature, inseparable from the true nature of all that is. We shift out of our ego identity into awareness itself: clarity and openness. Love, compassion, and wisdom spontaneously arise. As we do this meditation, this becomes more clear and actual. We begin to realize the difference between ego consciousness, the witness, and awareness, and we become able to shift from ego consciousness more easily.

For the purposes of the Love on Every Breath meditation, resting in witness consciousness and resting in awareness itself are both very beneficial. These are both helpful in daily life as well. When we rest our mind in either of these ways, we become more conscious of what is going on with our thoughts and actions. This is illustrated well by a student of mine, Michael, who is a longtime spiritual practitioner. Recently, Michael was betrayed by a close friend, Harry, who went back on certain promises that greatly affected Michael's life. Michael told me that normally he would be furious and his mind would be detailing all the ways Harry is a terrible, immature person. But, Michael said, he doesn't want to have his mind filled with negative thoughts. So instead, he has been taking time to meditate, to focus on settling and grounding in himself, in order to understand how this has freed him and how it is opening the door for a new life. Michael has also noticed how compassion for Harry has been spontaneously arising in his mind.

57

Philosophical Underpinnings

As I've mentioned, nothing truly exists. But neither does it not exist. Truth is beyond polarities. It is beyond dualities. The Buddha said that all that we perceive is like a dewdrop, a rainbow, a mirage. A dewdrop is impermanent; a rainbow and a mirage are illusory. These phenomena appear but are lacking in true existence. Nevertheless, they appear. This is the metaphor the Buddha used to help us understand the nature of reality. The nature of what is, is complete openness, the womb of the Great Mother who births all things and is never separate from the infinite totality. This openness in its true nature is awakened awareness. Gradually, through time spent in alert, mindful meditation, we come to have glimpses of our awakened awareness. These glimpses may feel quite ordinary: for example, a sense of well-being, of spaciousness, or feeling our basic goodness, our heartfelt wish for things to go well for others and ourselves. As our meditation practice continues and everything settles, as our conceptual overlay lets go, we are able to open into spaciousness, into relaxed transparency. In wakefulness, we are not grasping at anything or pushing anything away. We can open into our basic goodness whenever we remember to. Eventually, we come to realize the lack of separation between ourselves and all that is, and we come to realize the truth of what is.

58 On the path to full awakening through contemplation and meditation and the integration of the witness in daily life, sudden spiritual leaps in consciousness can bring our neurotic patterns into sharp relief. Students have recounted this to me many times — suddenly their mental and behavioral patterns reveal themselves clearly. At first, they report, they can't do much more than stare at these patterns. Then they begin to take responsibility for them, to see how they can make new choices, and to skillfully work through the unwholesome habits in daily life. If we stay with our conscious experience, we can release our old fixations while liberating old wounds and distorted beliefs about ourselves and others.

Twenty-five centuries of Buddhist meditation have confirmed that liberating wisdom comes from nonconceptual awareness. Our thinking mind will not lead to realization. The wisdom that brings liberation arises from our direct experience, a direct recognition that becomes direct knowingness. One reason for this is that, when we shift into nonconceptual awareness, we drop our ego identity project, and for the time being, we drop our ego strategies. We drop having to be a person, having to show up in a particular way, and having to be a particular kind of somebody. Just shifting from thinking to resting in awareness gives us relief. As we become familiar with resting our mind, the clarity of our perception increases and the capacity to choose what to focus on increases. Witness consciousness stabilizes as we directly observe our experience. Gradually, our attention becomes more and more like a powerful searchlight with which we can see what is. We develop the capacity to gaze directly at and into our experience, gazing both at the witness and at what is seen. Gradually, this leads to the realization of shunyata — or emptiness, as we call it in English — and the nonduality of subject and object becomes clear.

Realization of shunyata can occur in a flash. However, truly understanding and integrating this into our moment-to-moment experience takes time and requires real commitment. His Holiness the Dalai Lama told a story about the founder of his lineage, Tsangkapa. Even after having a powerful vision of the Bodhisattva of Wisdom, Manjusri, in which Tsangkapa achieved profound realization, he needed to keep studying and meditating in order to fully understand emptiness and dependent origination.* Having great insight is not enough. It does, however, give us a glimpse of what is possible. We have to be able to abide in genuine reality in order to actualize realization. Then we need to remember to do so even when our habitual patterns throw us into an ego reaction. We

---

* Dependent origination is the teaching from the Buddha that all phenomena are dependent on other phenomena as their cause. This is closely related to the Buddha's teaching on the causes of suffering and the causes to cease suffering.

need to be able and willing to get back on the horse. Realization needs to become stable. Finally, with great consistency, realization becomes fully integrated. The full actualization of wisdom, along with the blossoming of all positive qualities, is what is meant in Buddhism by complete awakening.

Over time with insight into the true nature of mind, we let go into shunyata, into our unchanging true nature, and into the union of awareness-emptiness. When the realization of the emptiness of self and other occurs, we are no longer in terror because we know that we are deathless. Through meditation and study, we gradually come to understand the nature of who we truly are and the nature of reality. These are not separate or different. Our true nature is not separate from another's, or from the nature of all that is. Our tendency is to split our experience into the duality of self and other, so it takes us time to understand that reality is not dual. Not only is it nondual, but from a Buddhist point of view the material world arises in consciousness: It is consciousness or awareness manifesting itself in a variety of forms — such as humans, nature, buildings, and so on. For example, everything I experience arises in my awareness. It is inseparable from my awareness. It seems like it is separate from me, but this is simply a habit of dualistic perception because of what the Buddha called our fundamental ignorance. Our consciousness is nonsubstantial — empty, yet everything arises in it in a very vivid way. Our meditation practice is a process of letting go into open awareness, letting go of concepts, and letting go into what is, fresh, open, clear.

In Mahayana Buddhism, the illusory phenomena are embraced with love and are interacted with through compassion and skillful means. Realization of the illusory nature of phenomena stirs our compassion and love for all beings. We care about all beings and love them universally. We want to actively engage in liberating ourselves and others from suffering, which is felt so acutely. This conviction led to the development of love and compassion meditation practices like Love on Every Breath.

Genuine reality points to that which is the unchanging, nondual essence of reality and mind. All phenomena have the same true nature and manifest inseparably as the union of form and emptiness. Phenomena, or the form aspect of our experience — whether our body, another being, nature, or the world — are ever-changing. Our bodies grow, getting stronger and bigger, and then eventually they age and deteriorate. The circumstances of our lives change in many ways — we learn, we work, we change jobs, we move into and out of relationships, loved ones pass away, and so on. Even the mountains, seemingly changeless from our perspective, change over time. Phenomena or appearances arise due to causes and conditions. Letting go and resting in formless awareness allows a reset in which new seeds, aligned with who we truly are, can be planted and nourished.

Issues That Can Arise When
Resting in Open Awareness

Resistance to meditating is familiar to all meditators. This is one of the main obstacles to practice. Usually, it manifests most strongly when we are moving toward the cushion. Suddenly, I may realize that I have forgotten to take out the trash. It's Thursday and the garbage must go out. I decide to do that first, and while taking out the trash, I notice that the garden is really dry, and it is supposed to be a hot day! I try to turn the water on, but I can't remember how to override the automatic irrigation system. So I place a call to the irrigation expert, and so on, until pretty soon the forty-five minutes I had set aside for meditation are gone. I console myself that I can meditate tomorrow. Of course, some chores are important and must be taken care of, but we need to keep our meditation time nonnegotiable.

Avoiding or resisting spiritual practice arises for many reasons, but there are common threads. We might feel intimidated by the idea of meditation, thinking, *My mind is too busy; I will never be able to do this.* One part of us might be determined to meditate, while another part may feel: *No way, I might lose my initiative if I simply let go and sit. If I'm meditating, I'm not getting anything done.* Or we might wonder, *Is it really okay to take time for myself?* These types of thoughts are often semiconscious. Many times we don't even know why a part of us doesn't want to meditate. Underneath these thoughts and feelings is often fear of some kind. Usually people need to exert extra willpower in order to just start meditating. One lama I know says, "You might as well just put out two cushions for your meditation sessions — one for you and one for your resistance. It will accompany you a lot of the time." That is, it's important to acknowledge any resistance: Give it some space, and move on with the meditation.

As our meditation becomes more of a daily habit, new patterns form. If we treat our daily meditation as nonnegotiable, like brushing our teeth, this can help — the same way a child might resist going to school until she realizes school is unavoidable, and so she settles down and accepts going every day. Meditating with others once a week or more is also helpful. Somehow, if we have a schedule to meditate with others, the ego often relaxes into the program. In a group, the combined intention of the meditators supports each individual to do it. Being accountable to our group, even if we only meet with them once a week, can help sustain our commitment to meditate.

Another option is to take some time off the cushion to inquire into the resistance. Sit quietly and ask yourself, *What is coming up for me?* Without trying to analyze it, simply listen carefully to what answer pops up. Keep questioning. Ask yourself, *Tell me more.* Don't reject any response. Just listen and keep inquiring. Responses that arise from the subconscious often don't make sense initially, but in my experience, if we keep following the threads without judgment, it all eventually becomes clear. An important point is to meet yourself with kindness, be present with your human self, just like you would be patient and kind with a small child you care about. Criticizing yourself simply adds to the difficulty.

We may think, *These instructions are too nebulous, too abstract, and besides, I don't know how to let go!* The instructions are abstract because they are trying to point to something that we need to discover for ourselves. Letting go is a skill that we need to develop. First, we can catch the times when we let go naturally, like when we drop onto the couch after a hard day at the office, when we reach our hiking destination and take a break, or when we lounge on our towel at the beach. If we consciously stay present during these experiences, we can see that we do know how to let go, but we need to cultivate this ability so that we can employ it anytime.

Another issue that often arises more specifically with this step is that the ego can feel afraid of disintegrating or dissolving. The ego has worked hard since early childhood to create a strategic operating structure. It can feel threatening to the ego to engage in spiritual practice. If we treat ourselves with kindness, it's easier for the ego to feel comfortable and learn

63

to relax with the process. Nothing bad is going to happen! We are not going to suddenly lose ourselves or dissolve into nothingness. The ego eventually learns that it doesn't have to be in charge all the time. It learns that it's nice to have a break!

Trying to keep everything in its own compartment is another issue in our spiritual work that can come up. For example, we might have our spiritual work in its own box that doesn't integrate with the rest of our life. Many times, clients have described to me a father who was abusive at home to his wife and children but who acted like a model citizen out in the world. People at their church and in the larger community thought he was wonderful. In different ways, we may also keep different parts of ourselves compartmentalized, so that we show a different face at church, at work, in the community, and at home. Resting in openness comes right up against this hypocrisy and compartmentalization. The ego is trying to do what's best for us, but the ego lacks essential information. It formulated its strategies at a young age. The early experiences we have gone through develop our core beliefs, and then we operate on that basis. We need to be willing to bring awareness to ourselves, inquiring deeply into our operating system and what is underneath it. Over time we see our core beliefs, and when we see and understand their erroneous nature, we can release them. This is a process that takes time and commitment.

As we become more familiar with meditation, we can drop into a less-triggered, less-reactive, more-skillful way of being whenever we are upset. Our activity can become more potent through openness, unbiased intelligence, and love. We can see new possibilities. As we train on the cushion, our mind gets used to new ways of perceiving, new ways of being, and an increased presence. As we integrate our meditation into daily life, it increasingly manifests in our moment-to-moment flow of experience and is carried into the whole of our lives. We act with more love, compassion, and wisdom.

In the Love on Every Breath meditation, Resting in Open Awareness refreshes us and provides open space for the next steps of the meditation, during which we engage in a creative meditative process — utilizing visualization, breath, prayer, and mantra as the meditation unfolds. Alternating in our meditation between formlessness and form is a process used in Vajrayana that helps loosen our clinging to phenomena. Clinging increases our tension, and so when we let go, our experience lightens up. Our habitual patterns and conditioning can transform and liberate, helping us realize the nonduality of form and emptiness. One of the other benefits is that it prepares us for death, for the time when our body drops away and we become solely mind.

COMPLETE MEDITATION
Step 1: Resting in Open Awareness

Sit comfortably to meditate, with your back upright. Have your eyes open and slightly downcast. Let go of thoughts of the past, present, and future. When thoughts arise again, let go of them, again and again.

Join your attention with your breath. Bring your attention inward and feel the sensations in your body. Let yourself come fully into contact with yourself, with your body and your emotions. Do not speculate about what is. Simply open to observe, feel, and connect with what is manifesting in the moment. As you continue to connect, breathe into your experience and let your mind settle. Rest in awareness, openness, and sensation inseparable.

When you are ready, allow your awareness to gradually radiate out to include your entire body and what is present around you. Let go into openness. Let the mind be like the sky. Perceptions and thoughts, like birds, do not disturb the sky. The sky does not chase after or judge them. They simply are there, and then they are gone. Let everything be; let the mind rest at ease in openness. Keep consciously breathing into your experience and relaxing, keeping your mind at ease, open, and resting in the vividness of your experience.

ON-THE-SPOT MEDITATION
Step 1: Resting in Open Awareness

Let go of thoughts. Let everything be as it is. Let the mind rest at ease in openness. When thoughts arise, let go of them, again and again.

Keep consciously breathing into your experience and relaxing, keeping your mind at ease, open, and focusing on stillness and the vividness of your experience.

Seeking Refuge
in Awakened Sanctuary

The winds of God's grace are always blowing,
it is for us to raise our sails.

— RAMAKRISHNA

*T*he Episcopalian diocese in the San Francisco Bay Area, where I grew up, was liberal and humanitarian, as it continues to be today. For me, the church was a place that promoted the values of love and the equality of everyone in our human family. I took seriously the prayers for peace and justice for people all over the world. I was taught both in the church and by my parents that those who had more, both in terms of education and financial resources, had an opportunity to joyfully work on behalf of others. I was taught to care for others as much as for myself. These values are also the basis of the bodhisattva path that I have traveled as an adult.

The church was also a place of refuge and nourishment for me spiritually. The priests and teachers created a space that was free of dogmatism, free of interference, and free of disturbance. This allowed me to connect on my own with the mystical stream of Christianity. This was incredibly nourishing and sustaining for me. I never even considered telling anyone about my experiences and feelings. I took them for granted as completely normal and private. As I look back, I am profoundly grateful for the spiritual transmission I received directly, without human intermediaries. By this I mean that, from my childhood, I simply opened myself to God and to Jesus during Holy Communion. I had my own experience of what the words we were saying meant. I had my own experience of God, of Jesus, and eventually, in my early adulthood, of Mother Mary. The priests in our church taught the Bible and Christianity from the point of view that everything in the teachings is symbolic of a deeper meaning. They elucidated their understanding of the deeper meanings, teaching us that it is by opening to the deeper meaning that we hear the true message of the sacred texts. They taught that we can each have our own relationship to God and Jesus and that no priest is needed to do so. I also was taught that God was a formless, ever-present, loving, and wise presence, infinite in scope. My childhood connection to Jesus and Mary continues to this day.

My idea and experience of God as a child and young person is not too different from what I came to understand as an adult through Buddhist study and meditation. In Buddhism, the Sanskrit term *prajnaparamita* literally means the "perfection of wisdom." This is formless, ever-present, all-pervading wisdom, but it is also personified as a female Buddha, as Prajnaparamita, the Great Mother, since in the Mahayana, which Tibetan Buddhism is part of, wisdom is seen as feminine: the realization of emptiness. Love and compassion are seen as the masculine aspect, yet inseparable from the

70

feminine. In Tibetan thangka paintings, the female and male are often depicted in physical intimate union, facing each other, signifying the union of the feminine and masculine aspects. Emptiness is love, love is emptiness. So I did not feel any real change in my experience between my notion of the Christian God and what is called "genuine reality" in Buddhism.

Practicing
Seeking Refuge in Awakened Sanctuary

Step 2 in Love on Every Breath is to seek refuge and to ask for sanctuary. In an ordinary sense, refuge means a place to be safe and protected from danger. A refuge is a sanctuary. While we all seek refuge, what we seek refuge from is unique to our lives. It may be from a lack of fulfillment or safe housing, from anxiety, war, abuse, violence, discrimination, an unhappy relationship, or any number of challenges.

What these all have in common is suffering, be it extreme or mild, physical, emotional, or mental. It doesn't help to compare our suffering to that of others. All of us want relief. We all want sanctuary. There comes a point for many of us where we realize that our life is not working and we long for more security, freedom, joy, peace, and love. We seek to find out if there is any true refuge. We explore if we can live differently, if a shift is possible. Like a refugee who awakens one day, yearning for safety, freedom, and peace, and who realizes that they must leave their homeland, you now resolve to leave the way you have lived and seek a different way of life, regardless of whether you know what this will look like or whether it is even possible. In the meditation, refuge is a metaphor that describes this change in orientation.

Who or what do we take refuge in? The Buddha distinguished between refuge that is genuine and apparent.

Apparent refuge gives us a kind of refuge for a period of time, but it is impermanent. This may be the refuge of a good job, home, relationship, income, or community. These kinds of refuge are important for us as human beings, but they are not reliable in the long term, as they do not bring us permanently out of suffering. They have a way of changing or deteriorating, and then they are no longer a refuge; in addition, we cannot bring these with us when we die. It is valuable to find a refuge that we can always go to, even at the time of death. The Buddha taught followers to take genuine refuge in him as a demonstration of liberation, of full awakening. He taught us to take refuge in the Dharma, the teachings and practices that make up the path, and in the realized "Noble Sangha" as guides and for inspiration. Ultimately, our refuge is in the true nature of who we are; this is our awakened sanctuary.

72

The relentless fury of the pounding waves in the infinite ocean of samsara.

SANCTUARY OFFERED

Illustration credit © Gwen Gordon

The Six-Fold Refuge: The Three Jewels

In Vajrayana, this awakened sanctuary is conceived as a "six-fold refuge," which consists of "three jewels" and "three roots." The Buddha, the Dharma, and the Noble Sangha are the three jewels that support us in this journey. The three roots are the masters of the lineages, the *yidams* (or awakened beings who embody particular qualities), and the dakinis, dakas, and protectors (or embodiments of awakened protection).

In this book's Love on Every Breath meditation, I offer the option to invoke just the three jewels or to also call upon the three roots as well; it's up to you.

The First Jewel: The Buddha

On the surface, seeking refuge in the Buddha means to take refuge in an awakened being who demonstrated that it is possible for human beings to fully awaken and be liberated from suffering. Buddha showed the path, and we can follow his example. We can call upon Buddha and take refuge in his awakened presence from the storms of our lives, from our ignorance that results in suffering, from overwhelm, from depression, from despair. When someone fully awakens, their consciousness is freed. They do not disappear into nothingness. They can hear and respond to us when we call upon them. Buddha reflects back to us the wisdom and love that abides as the essential nature of who we truly are. In short, we take refuge from *samsara*, which is what Buddhism calls the cyclic realm of our habitual patterns and the effects of our ignorance, the root cause of our suffering. We can open to the possibility of our awakening, of uncovering, purifying, and coming into who we truly are. We can begin to open to our intrinsic wisdom and love through feeling or seeing it in another and feeling the part in us that resonates with this. Our qualities of kindness, patience, courage, strength, generosity, skillfulness with others, realization, and so forth can emerge and fully blossom.

This also means taking refuge in our inner awakened nature. Buddha showed us the way to uncover and realize who we truly are. We take refuge in the fundamental goodness that we see arising in ourselves and others, however much it is covered over or disguised. Modern science has begun to confirm that there is innate goodness at the core of human beings. Emma Seppälä writes, "A study by Lara Aknin and colleagues at the University of British Columbia shows that even in children as young as two, giving treats to others increases the givers' happiness more than receiving treats themselves." Dacher Keltner at the University of California, Berkeley, coined the term "compassionate instinct," which posits that compassion is innate and natural.[7]

Our intrinsic awakened nature is obscured by the pervasiveness of our misunderstanding. This confusion regarding our true nature leads us to take the self as truly existent and separate from others. Because of this, we tend to evaluate everything moment to moment. We try to get and hold on to what we deem helpful or pleasurable and push away what we consider negative. Eventually, our many strategies become like well-worn pathways we travel unconsciously most of the time.[8] Our usual approach is based on misunderstanding the reality of what is, so ultimately it doesn't work. It seemingly works at times when we accumulate what we want, whether it be getting our desired job, relationship, home, friends, children, car, or all of the above and more. However, not only are these favorable conditions impermanent, but undesired factors can suddenly enter and cause havoc with our carefully constructed life. So our usual approach doesn't bring us inner peace or satisfaction. Our girlfriend gets together with our best friend, our boss leaves and we no longer enjoy going to work, our kids get in trouble. We become used to our comfortable surroundings and no longer appreciate them. We take our spouse for granted and fixate on their flaws, our body ages and declines, and so on. This is why on the path of awakening we take refuge in the Buddha who actualized ever-present wisdom.

In Love on Every Breath, like all Buddhist tantric meditations, the awakened beings dissolve into ourselves as a way of our feeling awakened presence inside. It is a way of realizing our inseparability with our mentors and with awakened body, speech, and mind. It is a way of realizing that we are not separate from the vast true nature of all that is. Duality gives way to nonduality. Form dissolves into formlessness.

The Second Jewel: The Dharma

The second object of refuge is the Dharma. In Sanskrit the word *dharma* literally means "truth." Within a Buddhist context, it refers to the teachings and practices that have come down to us from Buddha and the masters of the lineages who followed him. This is often referred to as Buddha Dharma.

We take refuge in the spiritual teachings and practices that can lead us to uncover our awakened nature. We engage in the path. We listen to teachings and philosophy, contemplate their meaning, and see if they resonate with us. If they do, we apply them in our meditation and daily life, and their inner meaning will be illuminated in our practice over time.

The inner refuge of the Dharma is our understanding and realization of truth, which opens up through our study, contemplation, meditation, and all our spiritual practices. As we study, follow, and apply the wisdom of the Dharma on our path, realization occurs. Usually, realization occurs in stages. We don't know when this will happen, but if we engage sincerely, it will occur eventually. I have seen this over and over again — from my initial surprise when realization occurred to seeing the same happen for my students. Our spiritual practices help us navigate through turbulent times, leading us to safer waters of greater peace, joy, and love. As we continue in this process, our understanding broadens and develops into knowledge that is based not on concepts or beliefs but rather on direct insight.

The Third Jewel: The Noble Sangha

The third object of refuge is what are called the Arya Sangha. The term *arya* is Sanskrit for "noble," and the Noble Sangha are those individuals who have attained a significant level of liberation and realization. Historically, in the Theravadin Buddhist tradition, widely practiced in Thailand, Burma, and Sri Lanka, this category included those monastics who reached the level of "stream entrant," *sotapanna* in Pali. This is defined as being free from three fetters: believing the self to be truly existent, clinging to rites and rituals, and having doubt or indecision. In Mahayana, it is defined as those who have reached the path of insight and beyond in the bodhisattva five-paths schemata. This corresponds to the first of ten stages of the bodhisattva path to full awakening. Arriving to the path of insight and the first *bhumi*, the stage of the path called Supremely Joyful, means that the nature of mind has been realized directly as it is — not just as an experience, but there is real understanding that will not fade. One has certainty, and this brings great joy and the ability to be of great benefit to beings. The perfection, or *paramita*, of generosity is fully actualized.

With the third jewel, we take refuge in the mentors and companions on the path, and we take refuge in our interconnectedness with the whole. We open to the entirety of our experience, knowing that it is simply our experience, trusting that we do not need to fear its unfolding, trusting that we can meet it and be present with it without fear.

Nowadays, many people think of the Noble Sangha as the community of people they study and practice with. These people can be companions who support us, as we all rub up against one another, learning and transforming through our relationships. However, if not awakened, these people are not true objects of refuge. They can disappoint or betray us or cease to be a Dharma friend. The idea of taking refuge is to look to that which is truly dependable and not subject to change.

The Six-Fold Refuge: The Three Roots

In order to understand the three roots, it can be helpful to first discuss the three *kayas*. *Kaya* is an honorific term that means "awakened body" in Sanskrit. *Dharmakaya* literally translates as the "truth body of enlightenment." This refers to the full realization of a Buddha. It is formless. Out of love and compassion, awakened mind takes form in order to be of more benefit to sentient beings, and this manifests as the two form *kayas*. These are *sambhogakaya*, or the body of rapture, communication, and awakened energy; and *nirmanakaya*, the body of emanation, a being with an actual physical body. *Sambhogakaya* beings have subtle bodies of light and form. We can encounter them in dreams or visions, and we can call upon them and imagine them as present. The latter eventually move beyond imagination, and we can feel their presence. *Nirmanakaya* beings can take birth as a human being or another kind of sentient being. In the Jataka tales of Buddha Shakyamuni's previous lives as a bodhisattva, he sometimes took birth as an animal. As I mentioned earlier, the Dalai Lama and the Karmapa are examples of *nirmanakaya* emanations of Chenrezig (or Avalokitesvara), the Bodhisattva of Compassion who has a primary role in many Mahayana sutras, most famously in what is commonly known as the Heart Sutra (or *Prajnaparamita*). Once a being attains full and complete awakening, they are fully liberated. After they leave the physical body, they are able to emanate or incarnate in one form, or more, out of love and the intention to be of benefit to others. Dhyani Buddhas, the buddhas that arose spontaneously from the *dharmakaya*, can also emanate. From a Buddhist point of view, Jesus was a *nirmanakaya* manifestation of God. This way of understanding various spiritual beings can be used across traditions.

Whether we believe in all this does not matter. As the Buddha said, "Test everything I say. Don't believe it just because I have said it." There is nothing we need to believe in Buddhism, but if we study and meditate on a Buddhist path, we can be open and see what unfolds in our experience. Now that we have clarified the three *kayas*, let's move to the three roots.

The First Root: The Masters of the Lineages

The first of the three roots are the gurus, lamas, or masters of the lineages who have actualized and transmitted their realization. These people are the human link through the centuries all the way back to the Buddha. They may be alive now,

and be a very personal link for us, or they may be histori-
cal figures that we can connect with. They can be valuable
as inspiration. Their stories give us archetypal examples of
the various joys and challenges that can happen on the spiritual path. This can be a helpful encouragement, as we often
think that our struggles and shortcomings are personal to us.
When we see that realized masters have struggled with the
same things that we struggle with, it heartens us, and we can
develop greater acceptance and compassion for ourselves.

The question of gurus and spiritual teachers is a complex
subject. The Buddhist tradition emphasizes that we need to
investigate a person thoroughly before taking them on as our
teacher. If we are studying intellectually with them, then this
investigation may be simply looking into their teaching cre-
dentials. But if we want a teacher in the sense of a mentor or
guru, then we must observe the person carefully over time to
see if they know the teachings and meditations, if they have
integrated them or are working on integrating them into their
character — if they walk their talk, so to speak. The most
important quality is whether or not they embody loving-
kindness and compassion. As a colleague of mine once said
to me, "We cannot expect the teacher to have no shadow, but
we can expect them not to be run by it." Nevertheless, a mentor or guru whom we develop trust in over time can be very
valuable, as they are the ones who interact with us, teach us,
guide us, support us, and mirror back to us our true nature.
Through their example and presence they give us courage to
tread the path when it feels treacherous and intimidating.
They hold us in love through the challenges of our lives. They
may give us the profound essential instructions for realizing
true nature. So, if we have a teacher like this, we can include
them in our Awakened Sanctuary meditation.

The gurus of the lineages, like the buddhas, symbolize our true nature and the dedication to truth, courage, perseverance, steadfastness, and love. They signify these qualities in ourselves, along with our spiritual inspiration and enthusiasm. Most importantly, they point to awareness itself, our inner guru, who is our ultimate guru.

The Second Root: The Yidams

The second of the three roots are the *yidams*, *sambhogakaya* beings who embody particular qualities of awakened body, speech, and mind. For example, the female Buddha Tara embodies the awakened feminine in action. Tara comes quickly when called upon. When we pray to her, she helps remove inner and outer obstacles, alleviates anxiety and fear, soothes us, nourishes us, is a model for us, and helps men and women discover the awakened feminine within. In Buddhist tantra,* we bring both the feminine and masculine sides within us into awakened actualization. Calling on and meditating on the *yidams* can help us grow spiritually and in our worldly lives. They help get us in touch with different awakened aspects of ourselves, like strength, courage, love, beauty, and wisdom. Meditating on the *yidams* is said to bring spiritual accomplishments (or *siddhis*). The process of meditating on them, first as distinct from ourselves, and then as inseparable from ourselves, helps to loosen clinging to our ego so we can open into our potential. This is why it is said that they bring spiritual accomplishments, which fall into two categories:

80

---

*   Tantra arose in both Buddhism and Hinduism during the first millennium CE. The dates are unclear. It was a movement away from fixed dualistic beliefs, such as the caste system in Hinduism. The Vajrayana is also called Buddhist Tantra or Tantrayana. Many of the important scriptures in Vajrayana Buddhism are called tantras, such as the Kalachakra Tantra that the Dalai Lama transmits and teaches.

(1) ordinary, such as those that come with yogic meditation practice, like clairvoyance and clairaudience; and (2) the supreme, which is enlightenment. Their awakened qualities such as wisdom, loving-kindness, strength, and courage help us to connect with these qualities inside of ourselves.

However, like others, the second root also means taking refuge in who we truly are, that is, awakened presence, and in the qualities of awakened mind. Wisdom and love shine forth as various capacities, such as the capacity to pacify conflict, enrich with education, heal, bring different people together in harmony, and fight against injustice. Praises and commentaries on the *yidams'* meditations speak of their qualities and symbolic meaning.

The Third Root: Dakinis, Dakas, and Protectors

The last category of the six-fold refuge includes the dakinis, dakas, and protectors. They are embodiments of awakened activity and communication. Their protective activity encompasses guarding the teachings of the Dharma, as well as protecting meditators from outer and inner obstacles. When we take refuge in the protectors, we activate this energy in our psyche, which serves to alert us to our unwholesome ego activity and unhelpful, persistent patterns. Their beneficial activity includes establishing supportive connections and conditions. Calling upon and taking refuge in the dakinis and protectors opens us to feeling beneficent threads of interconnection that can support us in our journey. They serve as a reminder to take care with our thoughts and actions, practicing patience, kindness, and generosity. They remind us to have integrity with ourselves and others.

Internally, this means taking refuge in the idea and experience that our obstacles on the path are transformed by our attitude and by how we approach them. If we can approach our challenges with flexibility, an open mind, and a willingness to learn and grow, this creates auspicious interconnections between our world and us. We can turn our challenges, struggles, and obstacles into the path of awakening. In this way, they become fuel for liberation.

Turning Adversity into the Path

A student of mine demonstrated an example of difficulties turning into auspicious interconnections. He was dying of AIDS when effective medical treatment emerged just in time to save his life. A few years later, he came down with cancer that went throughout his body and into his bones. He decided to spend his remaining time on this earth volunteering as a river-rafting guide and mentor to kids. No matter what brought the children to the river, the man became an uncle to all of them: disadvantaged, rich, healthy, disabled — whatever their circumstances. He saw their inherent goodness and their inherent beauty. He challenged them, joked with them, and loved them. He facilitated the growth of their own joy, resilience, and community. He experienced great satisfaction and joy watching people transform. He chose not to focus on his own pain, but rather to focus on helping others. He gave talks to students at local high schools about sex and drugs. One of his doctors had him give talks to the hospital's resident doctors to help them understand a patient's point of view. The last years of this man's life became deeply meaningful, and coincidentally or not, he outlived his prognosis by many years. He rose to the challenge posed by his illness: to evaluate his life and live his last years in the most meaningful way he could, bringing him great joy and purpose.

There are many approaches to turning pain into the path of awakening. We can bring our emotions into our daily meditation. This allows them to settle and release. Our emotions can be brought into visualization and mantra practice as fuel for our meditation. This transforms and liberates them into pure energy. We can see that others are suffering in much the same way as we do. We can practice Love on Every Breath for ourselves and others.

Ultimately, our obstacles and challenges are fully liberated when we can rest in their true nature and realize their inherent lack of intrinsic reality — they are phenomena appearing in our field of awareness, appearance-emptiness, not capable of interfering with us or harming us. When we rest in openness with our experience, directly experiencing its vividness without pushing anything away or grabbing on to anything, we turn adverse conditions into training grounds, and transformation occurs for us on the path of awakening.

My First Taking Refuge

In my early twenties, before I met Kalu Rinpoche, I realized that I needed to connect with a teacher. I began to pray intensely to find my teacher. There was a beautiful old convent not far from where I was living at the time, and I would often go there to pray in front of the Mary statue. At some point after this, on a full moon in September 1977, a Sufi friend spent hours telling me about a highly respected Tibetan teacher and convincing me to go see him that night in San Francisco. Finally, I agreed. I was not thinking of the possibility that this might be my teacher. I just agreed to come along.

That evening, along with a medium-sized crowd, I found

myself in a large classroom in an old grammar school. Up front on the platform stage was a wizened teacher in maroon robes. As I sat and gazed at him, not thinking anything in particular, suddenly, in the depths of my heart, I knew this man was the teacher I had been longing for. I had never read about or had any contact with Tibetan Buddhism before. I had studied and meditated for some time with a Zen master, a student of Suzuki Roshi's named Bill Kwong who ran Sonoma Mountain Zen Center. And I had been sitting zazen at home every day for some years, along with doing hatha yoga, mantra, and prayer practice. I had studied and meditated in the Chishti Sufi tradition of Hazrat Inayat Khan. I had studied the Old Testament with a rabbi. I had studied early Christianity and also the Christian mystical tradition. All these traditions were for me a seamless fabric of incredible color, beauty, and texture. All this prior study and practice prepared me to meet and train with Kalu Rinpoche.

84

Then out of the blue, a lot of mucus started coming out of me — water started dripping from my eyes, I started coughing, and I had to blow my nose repeatedly. This lasted for about five minutes. It felt like a lot of old stuff, in the form of mucus, was leaving me. I was stepping into a new realm of shining light, playfulness, joy, and truth. It felt authentic, and I was speechless.

After a few minutes, I thought to myself, *Well, I guess whatever religion he is, is fine for me.*

Toward the end of my first evening with him, Rinpoche talked about the ceremony of taking refuge. Then he asked if anyone would like to participate. He explained that you did not need to give up any other religion in order to take the vows. I decided I wanted to do it, and I went up to sit on the stage at the foot of his traditional Tibetan lama seat. I looked around and noticed that there were five of us, all women, taking refuge. We recited the vows in Tibetan, repeating after him.

Near the conclusion of the ceremony, Rinpoche had the five of us come up one by one. He cut a tiny lock of our hair and gave each of us a name. Mine is Karma Palden Drolma. Karma in this context means in the family of the Karmapa* of the Kagyu lineage; this was the beginning of each name he gave, as he was traveling on behalf of Karmapa. He himself was a Kagyu lineage holder, as well as being the head of the Shangpa lineage, although I didn't know these details until later. Palden is translated as "glorious," and Drolma as Green Tara, the female Buddha. Six months after this, I continued studying and meditating with him at his monastery in Darjeeling in West Bengal, India.

In spite of the terrible weather in Darjeeling, being with Rinpoche was like being around a bright sun. His vast awakened love and humor dissolved all suffering, and it felt like being in a constant radiance of pure being.

The knowing that Kalu Rinpoche is my teacher has been unshakable for over forty years. In the words of author Roger Housden, "The word *knowing* is a verb and not a noun. It is a dynamic process, not a static something. It is a direct perception, unmediated by the thinking mind."[9]

Refuge Teachings

The practice of refuge or sanctuary as taught by the Buddha is common to all Buddhist lineages. The refuge that all Buddhists share is in the triple gem — the Buddha, the Dharma, and the Noble Sangha. We realize that our mental

---

* *Karmapa* literally means "man of action." In Sanskrit, *karma* is "action," and in Tibetan, *pa* is a male suffix.

acuity, our physical dexterity, our bank account, our present supportive conditions, even our relationships and community are not wholly sufficient. We turn toward the mystery and toward discovering what our true refuge is. We turn to those exemplary beings who embody love and wisdom, those who have passed on and those who are still with us in the flesh. We turn toward the teachings of truth and the spiritual practices that enable us to connect with our awakened nature, inseparable from all that is. Everyone who seeks this comes to know what is true for them in their heart and soul.

When we take refuge, it is important to understand that awakened beings such as Buddha Shakyamuni do not disappear into nothingness at the time of their death. Full and complete awakening, from a Buddhist point of view, is to achieve liberation. When this is actualized, phenomena such as death do not disturb or in any way limit our capacities. Rather, death frees our capacities from the limitations of the human body to benefit others in an infinite number of ways.

Through the awakened beings' infinite love and responsiveness, they come to us when we call upon them. We need to learn to be open and listen in silence to feel their presence. This develops over time as our sense of separateness lets go and our sense of possibility opens. The Tibetan teachers I studied with often said that the buddhas are holding out a hand to us, but unless we reach up and take their hand, no connection is made. If we take their hand, they can nurture and transmit to us. This is the same as a mother holding out her hand so her child can cross the street safely. This holding out of a hand, so to speak, holds true for saints or sages of the past as well. In their compassion, they also come when called upon. We often don't realize when this is happening. Our heart can attune through meditation and allow us to feel and connect. Awakened beings do not need to take form for their own sake. But they do so in order to help people. This is similar to the New Testament idea that God, who is formless, "so loved the world, that he gave his only Son, that whoever believes in him should not perish but have everlasting life." That is, formless God emanated from himself a human form, Jesus, in order to help others.

In our meditation on refuge, we reach out to various awakened beings, such as buddhas, sages, yogis, and yoginis of the lineages. We invite awakened mind and awakened presence into our space, and open ourselves to connect with it.

The step of Awakened Sanctuary is a meditation that is relevant for us all the way to full enlightenment. It increases our humility, openness, and support, and our access to enlightened transmission. Whether we have traveled the path for a long time or a short time, it can be comforting for the human part of us to find a sense of refuge in something beyond the self. It is helpful to feel held by another. Twelve-step programs have long made use of this truth by encouraging those in recovery to ask for help from their higher power and from their sponsor. The meetings are also set up so that there is strength and support from the group.

The American individualistic spirit — needing to be strong and capable and do everything by yourself — isn't all that realistic. It also reinforces the ego. The Buddhist yogis and yoginis, who were highly capable and certainly self-sufficient individuals, often spent years alone in caves, and yet they acknowledged that until awakening, we all need support, guidance, and love. The human part of us that feels overwhelmed thinks, *Oh my God, I have to do this whole thing myself.* We all need support.

When part of us feels vulnerable, unsafe, or emotionally

agitated, we can imagine a being whom we trust offering a container of safety, love, and awakened presence. One way I do it is to imagine Tara's hand on my head. Tara, the female Buddha, is known for removing fear and obstacles. She is adored in Vajrayana countries, and her meditation is done in all schools of Vajrayana Buddhism. When I imagine Tara's hand on my head, it feels as though the nectar of love and awareness flows out of her hand into me. I find it very soothing. You can simply call on the awakened beings in any situation: "Be with me, be right here with me." This is what the meditation on refuge is about.

Over time, we can connect more easily with our innate buddha nature or basic goodness. As we calm the mind and let go of unwholesome habits, it becomes easier to feel our innate qualities. The journey of study, reflection, and meditation opens us to our awakened essence. In the meantime, Buddhism, and Vajrayana in particular, uses our dualistic mind-set to go beyond dualism. It is easier for us to imagine someone other than ourselves being awakened. It can be easier to feel someone else's innate goodness and wisdom. We open to this possibility outside ourselves, as a way of connecting with the feeling of awakened presence, so that we can eventually feel it inside as well as outside.

We use the illusion of an awakened being separate from ourselves in order to move beyond the concept of dualism. In this case, it is the dualistic thinking that we are separate from enlightenment. Until nonduality is realized, fully incorporated, and actualized in ourselves, we can use a helping hand. We can benefit from opening to and feeling the transmission of awakened body, speech, and mind. This is valuable for us as human beings and is why all of Buddhism emphasizes the importance of refuge. Knowing this, instead of reaching for the false refuges when we're feeling down or upset, we can recognize our need and try to substitute the real thing.

Refuge is to return home to who we truly are, in the moment, and for the long run. Taking refuge activates true nature in us. It activates in our psyche the various qualities that are embodied in the objects of refuge. At the end of the meditation, when all the enlightened beings we have called upon and meditated on dissolve into us, we meditate on our inseparability with them. This softens our dualistic experience of awakened presence. Then we dissolve into openness as a way of letting go of form. This complete meditation is a powerful method for transforming our habitual view of self. Refuge practice strengthens and develops our capacity, confidence, and courage. This is like learning to rock climb. At first we train with an expert. They explain what to do and make sure we are doing it correctly. We begin in less-challenging situations, like training in a gym, until we get the hang of it, but we don't try to scale El Capitan in Yosemite until we are fully qualified, and our confidence and courage are up for it.

89

Issues That Can Arise during Awakened Sanctuary

Doubt is one issue that can arise. Many of us, subconsciously or consciously, do not believe that Shakyamuni Buddha is still present with us today. We may believe that the Buddha awakened, but we may not realize what this means. We may not understand that the complete awakening, which the Buddha achieved and described, liberates one fully from illusion, from limitation, and from the constraints of time and space. We may not think this is possible. We may think that this is storytelling hyperbole. We may think that the whole idea of awakened beings sounds like superstition or wishful thinking. But enlightenment does not mean you die forever and disappear into nothingness. This is similar in other traditions as well. For example, Jesus is no longer a human being on this earth, but that does not mean that he is gone. Through calling upon him, praying to him, we can connect with him. So we may feel that the Buddha is gone, but is this what we believe enlightenment means? What is the point of awakening if we disappear?

Another issue that can arise is that asking for help may be repugnant. Or we may feel that we should be able to do everything for ourselves. We may feel that asking for help is a sign of weakness. Many of my teachers spent years alone in caves in the high mountains of Tibet. This is not the path of a wimp. This is not a path that works for wishful think-

ers. Yet Kalu Rinpoche, like all my Tibetan teachers who had spent many years in retreat, advocated again and again that we deeply and sincerely call upon the awakened beings for support, transmission, and blessings. Once when a few of us were sitting with Kalu Rinpoche, someone asked, "What is the tune for the guru yoga mantra?" He cried out (the only time I ever heard him raise his voice), "Lama, help!" Then he said that we should yell it so loud that our neighbors knock on the wall to quiet us.

Part of the illusion that keeps us feeling cut off from awakened or divine presence is the belief that we are our own separate islands — skin-encapsulated egos who must do everything by ourselves. In America, pulling oneself up by one's own bootstraps is highly valued. We may think that it is weak to want or need the help of others: "I don't need anybody to help me." This is a fixated position that reinforces the sense of "I," the sense of a separate self, and reinforces an ego belief that "I am alone." This can lead to the ego feeling burdened, overwhelmed, and unsupported. But this is not the case. Knowing how to give and accept help, to receive and give support, is psychologically healthy. We are interconnected, social beings.

A mystery of reality is that we are individuals and at the same time not disconnected from one another. We are inseparable from everything that is, and we are also unique. Our consciousness is not separate from the totality of what is and we also have individual consciousness. This mystery goes beyond paradox — beyond the duality of being this way or that way.

We may feel that we are unworthy of attention and love. In this case, we need to see that everyone is equally worthy. Everyone has buddha nature at the core of who we are. Our innate primordial goodness may be very hard to detect in the dung heap of our ignorance, but it never is gone entirely. In our disconnection from who we truly are, we may think, *How could it be possible that they care for me?* These issues are often best addressed with a combination of spiritual practice and psychotherapy, or the process of personal inquiry where we unwind unwholesome patterns and release old beliefs that bind us to suffering even though they are not true.

Often, as we go further on the path, our core psychological issues come up more and more. This may sound discouraging, but it is not. They come up in order to be liberated from our stream of being.* When an issue comes up, we have an opportunity to apply the Dharma teachings and meditations to free ourselves, to recognize that we are really not our issues.

91

---

* "Stream of being" is the translation of a Tibetan term meaning our deathless awareness and the patterns and karma that are carried along with it through lifetimes.

COMPLETE MEDITATION
Step 2: Seeking Refuge in Awakened Sanctuary

Call upon the Buddha, the Dharma, and the Noble Sangha. See them appear in the sky in front of you. Ask for their support, guidance, and awakened transmission. Open to their presence, and imagine them responding to you with their great love and wisdom. Gradually, you will come to actually find sanctuary in their support, wisdom, and love.

Chant this refuge prayer three or seven times:

> *Until awakening I take refuge in the Buddha,*
> *the Dharma, and the Noble Sangha,*
> *By the merit of my acts of generosity and other*
> *awakening qualities,*
> *May I attain full awakening for the benefit of all beings.*

Or, if you wish, for the full Vajrayana version, in addition to the above, also call upon the gurus, the *yidams*, the dakas, the dakinis, and the protectors, and chant the following prayer:

> *I go for refuge to the glorious holy gurus.*
> *I go for refuge to the buddhas, the transcendent conquerors.*
> *I go for refuge to the sacred Dharma.*
> *I go for refuge to the Noble Sangha.*
> *I go for refuge to the assembly of dakas, dakinis, Dharma*
> *protectors, and guardians, all who possess the eye of*
> *awakened awareness.*

The enlightened beings dissolve into you. You become inseparable from them. Feel their blessing. Then let go and rest again in formlessness.

ON-THE-SPOT MEDITATION
Step 2: Seeking Refuge in Awakened Sanctuary

You can use this On-the-Spot version before any meditation in order to infuse your mind and space with enlightened energy, support, and guidance. You can use it when you are in a stressful situation and feel the need for support, such as before having a difficult conversation or when entering a new situation.

A few years ago I was turning left onto a busy boulevard when an SUV came hurtling around the bend. I realized there was no way to avoid being hit. In that split second, I called on the buddhas and opened to my connection with the inner refuge of true nature. This allowed me to let go into peace. I came to as the car was spinning, my head throbbing, but I felt relaxed and alert. Later I thought that my years of meditating had helped me let go into this moment and feel safe, despite the circumstances.

Call upon the Buddha, the Dharma, and the Noble Sangha. Ask for their support and guidance. Imagine them in front of you, responding with their great love and wisdom. Gradually, you will come to actually feel sanctuary in their support, wisdom, and love.

Pray to these beings for sanctuary. Open to a sense of connection and transmission from awakened presence.

The refuge beings dissolve into you, and you become inseparable from them. You and all that is dissolve into open space. Rest your mind in evenness, inseparable from openness.

STEP 3

Cultivating Awakened Mind

*Sometimes we get too angry with ourselves thinking
we ought to be perfect from the word go. But this being on earth
is a time for us to learn to be good, to learn to be more loving,
to learn to be more compassionate.*

— DESMOND TUTU

Step 3 of the meditation is Cultivating Awakened Mind, or what is also called Cultivating Bodhicitta. Bodhicitta is the heart essence of love, compassion, and kindness. It is the altruistic intention to awaken in order to be able to alleviate suffering and bring happiness to all beings, regardless of religion, gender, color, or ethnicity, whether human or animal. There are traditional prayers that you can use for this, such as the ones in meditation steps 2 and 3, or you can use your own words.

In this meditation, we delve deeply into our hearts and connect with the part of us that wants the best for everyone.

We open to and cultivate the full richness of our innate love and compassion for our loved ones and those with whom we identify, such as our family, our tribe, our country, or our type of people. We gradually expand to include others outside our usual circles. We gently open the door to the full glory of our innate love, extending it impartially and equally to all beings, including ourselves.

Can we imagine a world in which everyone's needs are met? In which everyone is healed, the clouds of our confusion lift, and we are all liberated from creating more suffering? Can we imagine us all living in cooperation, peace, and joy? This is the bodhisattva vision. On the path, as aspiring bodhisattvas, we pray to be of benefit to others. We commit to fully awaken, to actualize who we are in order to be able to truly help all beings.

This step in the meditation is to develop and affirm our altruistic intention for our meditation. We affirm that we are doing our meditation on behalf of all beings.

Integrating Bodhicitta into Daily Life

Spiritual practice does not only happen during meditation. Throughout each day, we can train ourselves to remember bodhicitta. For example, when we read the news in the morning, we can think: *I want to lead people out of suffering. I want to awaken to be able to make a difference.* We don't need to feel powerless. It often seems like things are going in the wrong direction, but love is stronger. Truth is stronger. If we continue to cultivate bodhicitta, it awakens our heart continuously so that our love and compassion get stronger in the face of any situation we meet. We bring wisdom into the mix by actively reflecting on what would truly be helpful.

It is said that Medicine Buddha, before his enlightenment, made a wish that he be able to heal those who are sick in body or mind. When he awakened, he became Medicine Buddha with the special quality of healing.

Opening our hearts to loving-kindness over time develops into unconditional love for ourselves and others. As we calm our mind and open our heart, our meditation clears what's in the way of us experiencing and, ultimately, embodying our innate buddha nature. The spiritual path gives us methods to transform our confusion into wisdom, our disdain or indifference into love. As we grow and work through our pain and uncover our innate radiant goodness, we increase our capacity to benefit others. Helping others brings us joy and happiness and even relieves stress. Research now confirms this.[10]

We work on not seeing ourselves as better or worse than any other being. We contemplate and feel the equality of all beings. Every one of us has buddha nature, that divine spark within, even if it is so obscured as to be unrecognizable. Realization brings the understanding of the fundamental equality and goodness of all beings. On the path we sometimes have breakthroughs where this experience shines through our ordinary mind, which is usually full of thoughts and concerns.

To fully embody the depth of our awakened love takes persistence in doing the spiritual practices that transform us. We must watch our mind throughout the day in order to let go of our grumpiness, our self-centeredness, our arrogance, and instead open into loving-kindness and compassion. The full radiance and expression of our innate goodness is liberated on the path when we let go of our small self-interest. This does not mean that we don't take care of ourselves — quite the contrary. We bring loving-kindness to ourselves as well.

Embodiment of Awakened Love

I had the blessing to study with some of the most highly realized Tibetan bodhisattvas of the twentieth and twenty-first centuries. They spent years in solitary retreats in caves, dedicating their lives to the bodhisattva path. A bodhisattva is one who has taken the bodhisattva vow — to awaken in order to liberate all beings from suffering. Bodhisattvas dedicate their lives to all beings. Following their long retreats, they dedicate themselves to working with students and being helpful in society. The bodhisattvas I studied with were completely at ease, regardless of the fact that they were all refugees, having fled the Chinese takeover of Tibet. They embodied boundless love and compassion.

One late afternoon in the swirling fog of the darkening light, when I was in Darjeeling studying with Kalu Rinpoche, I met him on the path between the temple and his quarters. I was distressed about the health of a monk who had been helping me, and I tried to communicate this to Rinpoche, so that perhaps he would do a Chöd ceremony for this monk. Rinpoche couldn't understand my very broken Tibetan, but with the utmost love, he reached out toward me and picked a spider off my shirt. I was overcome by this expression of his love and was bathed in it. He didn't understand what I was saying, but he reached out to me with utter compassion. Later, he found out what I had been trying to communicate and arranged a Chöd healing ceremony for the monk.

Several years later, I was in Greece during a trip around the world with the sixteenth Karmapa. After Karmapa's teaching, many people with challenging circumstances came one by one to his rooms to see him personally. Before they came in, Karmapa looked utterly exhausted. He was suffering from late-stage stomach cancer. Nevertheless, no one was turned away, and as soon as he saw people come in, his entire countenance changed, becoming filled with love and vitality. He reached out with so much interest and affection to each person who came to see him. It was so moving to experience his awakened love manifesting for those who needed it. I heard that he also demonstrated this quality when he was dying in a Chicago hospital. The medical staff reported that each time they would enter his room and ask how he was feeling, he would cheerfully respond that there was no problem and then immediately change the subject to how they were doing.

The Benefits of Cultivating Awakened Mind

As I've said, modern neuroscience has now found that altruism brings us happiness in addition to being a stress reliever.[11] This mirrors Buddhist teachings. The *Prajnaparamita* teaching on the innate purity of all sentient beings and of the infinite universe directly counters the Christian doctrine of original sin.* Whether we were taught about original sin or not, in Western cultures our psyche is permeated by the feeling that something is wrong with us — that there is some flaw at the core of who we are. Often, people feel a sense of shame deep inside — that we aren't good enough, or don't have what it takes, or are defiled. To open to the idea that we are all inherently good is a radical shift. Through our meditations and practice of loving-kindness and compassion, we gradually come into an experiential sense of our basic goodness.

---

* Matthew Fox has worked to transform this notion in Christianity by positing the concept of "original blessing" (which he describes in a book of the same name).

Love is the healing balm that eases and enriches our journey through life. It opens the door for us to recognize the equality and beauty of each being and ourselves. It brings joy and fulfillment into both our personal relationships and our relationship with ourselves. The Dalai Lama and Desmond Tutu discuss this in their book *The Book of Joy: Lasting Happiness in a Changing World*. Desmond Tutu says, "I mean simply to say that ultimately our greatest joy is when we seek to do good for others." Later, the Dalai Lama comments, "The best way to fulfill your wishes, to reach your goals, is to help others, to make more friends.... [S]how your genuine sense of concern for their well-being."[12]

As we develop our altruistic aspiration and engage in Love on Every Breath, we get more in touch with our fundamental goodness, our pure being. Indicative of our basic goodness is the spontaneous compassion that can arise when we witness someone in distress. Our true nature pops through in moments like this. The Buddha taught that ignorance of who we truly are, and our psychological strategies that follow, obscure our awakened nature.

We are like the full moon covered by clouds. The moon is never really gone; its light is just obscured. On a cloudy night, once in a while the clouds part and the brilliance of the moon reveals itself in all its glory. Once in a while, our innate pure being, love, shines through. In a crisis, we rush to help someone we don't know, or we are touched deeply by others' suffering and write a check for hurricane relief.

Recent research on infants supports the premise that our inborn nature is altruistic. One 2009 study summarized: "Human infants as young as fourteen to eighteen months of age help others attain their goals, for example, by helping them to fetch out-of-reach objects or opening cabinets for them. They do this irrespective of any reward from adults (indeed, external rewards undermine the tendency), and very likely with no concern for such things as reciprocation and reputation."[13]

As we cultivate universal love that is based on the equality and worthiness of all people, it sets our intention and motivation and the trajectory for our spiritual path and actions. Love on Every Breath helps us to actualize this. The bodhisattva intention to awaken on behalf of all sentient beings mirrors the reality that there is no separation between self and other. This elevates our meditation beyond a personal growth practice. We can train our minds to infuse every moment of life with uncontrived, unsentimental kindness. The Dalai Lama is a great example of this. He stays grounded in himself and present with others with steadfast loving-kindness.

Prajna and *Upaya*: Wisdom and Skillfulness

Our *prajna*, or "wisdom awareness," glimpses and then fully recognizes truth, gradually coming to fully embody wisdom and love. Compassion for all beings naturally arises when we realize true nature.

In Vajrayana, *upaya*, or "skillful means," are used to help us uncover innate wisdom and compassion and to work through and liberate our persistent unwholesome attitudes, behaviors, psychological issues, and the misunderstandings that obscure our true nature. Our development of skillful means helps us to be of benefit to others.

Engendering a broad, inclusive love for all beings is the basis of the Mahayana or bodhisattva path of meditation. Mahayana recognizes the illusory nature of what is: how things vividly appear and yet are empty of inherent self-identity. Yet we are taught, and my teachers surely demonstrated, not disdain or disregard for phenomena, but how to embrace what is with love. As I discussed earlier, genuine reality refers to the unchangeable, primordial purity and bliss-emptiness. True nature is the union of shunyata, or emptiness, and appearance, or presence. Phenomena appear to all our senses and to our minds, and yet they are a mirage. Genuine truth is inseparable from apparent truth. Apparent reality is what the Tao Te Ching calls the "ten thousand things," the world of multiplicity, change, and flux, the dream. In the words of Tilopa, the tenth-century Mahamudra master of the Kagyu lineage, "The past is but a memory, the future a fantasy, and the present moment vanishes when we try to grasp it."

And yet, as human beings, we need supportive conditions, food, water, air, and shelter in order to live. We are incredibly vulnerable. Earthquakes, floods, and guns can easily destroy us if we are in the wrong place at the wrong time. The bodhisattva understands this poignancy — how on the one hand we are deathless, and on the other hand we are always at risk. Therefore, love arises as the appreciation of the beauty of beings and their vulnerability. The path is the flowering of wisdom as we realize genuine truth, and the flowering of love as we embrace apparent reality. Wisdom and love are said in Dzogchen* to be the two wings of the bird that takes us to enlightenment: They are cultivated and yet revealed, as we discover who we truly are. So let us embrace life with love, and as one of my teachers, Khenpo Tsultrim Gyamtso Rinpoche, said, "Since you are all making movies, make a good one!"

------

* A Tibetan word meaning "great completion," Dzogchen is the highest system of teachings in the Nyingma Vajrayana lineage.

Be Aware of Other Motivations Besides Helping

It's important to examine our motivation to help in order to recognize and acknowledge any other agendas. For example, helping others can sometimes be more about protecting ourselves, such as trying to assuage our guilt about our privilege. Sometimes we help because we don't want confrontation, we don't want to ruffle somebody's feathers, or we want to be seen as loving and nice. Sometimes another person's suffering triggers our own suffering, so we try to fix their problems so that we can feel better. That's basic codependence. If we are ruminating on how we want to respond to something, it's helpful to try to sort through our motivations and identify what we are trying to accomplish.

Sometimes we leap to try to fix someone, or fix their life, because we are in pain. We can interfere when it is not actually our job (engaging in what Trungpa Rinpoche called "idiot compassion"). We need to give people the space to make their own assessments and decisions. That said, we don't want to try to avoid conflict at the expense of actually working things through. For example, when a family member is struggling with drug addiction, we might think it's helpful or compassionate to be "nice" and pretend no problem exists, thereby avoiding painful conflicts. However, ignoring problems does not solve those problems or help the other person.

We all need to be forgiven and to forgive. Being able to forgive is essential for our peace of mind and for healing our relationships. We need to develop our capacity to forgive. However, in order to be meaningful, this needs to be authentic. We need to be ready to forgive. We do not want to forgive before we have worked through our feelings of betrayal, anger, or hurt. This jumps to forgiveness when we are not there yet. It takes time to authentically process our feelings and come to true forgiveness in our hearts, especially if what has happened has been violent or destructive. If we quickly forgive before processing our profound pain and grief, in actuality we are not ready yet to forgive. This "idiot forgiveness" can also happen when we have an idea that we are supposed to be "spiritual." So we try to push our feelings under the rug in an effort to be forgiving.

It's imperative to be clear about our motivation to benefit others, to make sure what we do aligns with our values and integrity. When we are genuinely helping another instead of saving ourselves from discomfort, then we can authentically move forward with our compassion. When we broaden our intention to bring benefit to all others, instead of just to ourselves, our family, and our tribe, we align with our true nature — boundless love and liberating wisdom. This brings us joy. This is an important step on the spiritual path. We take a step toward nondual realization. If we want realization, but we do not want to open our heart, or are afraid to, then realization is not going to occur. The path of awakening requires both heart and courage.

Resolving the War Within

I grew up in an upper-middle-class, well-educated family. My father was successful. Our neighborhood was full of lawyers, CEOs, and politicians. Yet at thirteen years of age, I couldn't help noticing that my parents and my friends' parents were miserable. They had achieved the American Dream, but they were neurotic, they were drinking too much, and their marriages were falling apart. I remember thinking, *Something is wrong with this picture. These people have beautiful homes, families, jobs, money, and prestige, but they are not happy. They are miserable. There must be a different way to live my life.*

This led me, at age fourteen, to study the writings of people like Mahatma Gandhi, Yogananda, and Huston Smith. I also studied some of the Western philosophers and psychologists. When I tried psychedelics, my world as I knew it showed itself to be far more transparent, workable, and responsive than I could ever have imagined. Throughout my teens, I participated in groups and learned to meditate. As a fifteen-year-old in the late sixties, I worked as a summer volunteer on a campaign to stop the war in Vietnam. One day, after stuffing envelopes, I walked outside and thought, *The war is in me, too. This anger and aggression that fuels conflicts is in me, too. I need to work on resolving the war within me.*

Of course, at fifteen I had no idea what a long-term project this would be. It turns out that to truly bring myself to peace, to fulfillment, to a happiness that is not dependent on circumstances, is a major piece of work. Meditation, spiritual study, yoga, therapy, and inquiry work, along with a little help from my friends and family, have made an amazing difference in my internal landscape. We can endlessly try to create the good circumstances in our life, but without working on ourselves, we do not usually find real happiness. As it is said, this is like rearranging the chairs on the *Titanic*. Even if we are able to get everything lined up how we want it, something always goes awry. All that effort to get the chairs perfect, and the ship sinks.

Issues That Can Arise
in Cultivating Awakened Mind

Various kinds of resistance can arise to cultivating unbiased universal love. Once a student said to me, "I'm overwhelmed just thinking about bringing all beings to awakening. I'm going to be struggling forever, and I don't want that. I have plenty of my own suffering. How can I consider opening to others' sorrows? And besides, doesn't the bodhisattva vow state that we put off our awakening until all beings are awakened? That sounds miserable." I told her this is the very reason we strive to awaken — to free ourselves so we are able to benefit beings in a lasting way. Some people think that the bodhisattva vow means to put off awakening, but this is a misunderstanding of the teaching. Yes, it is sometimes written that bodhisattvas put off enlightenment until all beings are liberated. But it is not meant to be taken literally. It means that after awakening, a bodhisattva continues to manifest in the world in order to be of benefit. The bodhisattva vow is to awaken in order to be able to liberate all beings. Once you are fully awakened, not only are you free, but you have limitless skillful means with which to be of help. Here is an inspiring quote by Shantideva from his renowned text *The Way of the Bodhisattva*:

> *May I be a guard for those who are protectorless,*
> *A guide for those who journey on the road.*
> *For those who wish to go across the water,*
> *May I be a boat, a raft, a bridge.*
>
> *May I be an isle for those who yearn for landfall,*
> *A lamp for those who long for light;*
> *For all who need a resting place, a bed;*
> *For those who need a servant, may I be their slave.*
>
> *May I be a wishing jewel, the vase of plenty,*
> *A word of power and the supreme healing,*
> *May I be the tree of miracles,*
> *For every being the abundant cow.*

Just like the earth and the pervading elements,
Enduring as the sky itself endures,
For boundless multitudes of living beings
May I be their ground and sustenance.

Thus for every thing that lives,
As far as the limits of the sky,
May I provide their livelihood and nourishment
Until they pass beyond the bonds of suffering.[14]

Bodhisattva Path: Nondual Realization Is Simultaneous with Love

In awakening, we realize that essential nature is nondual — that our vivid awareness, appearance, and shunyata (or the reality that things do not truly exist in the way we think they do) are not separate. Myself and others are not separate, heaven and earth are not separate, *samsara* and nirvana are of one taste.* Phenomena may be unique and impermanent, but true nature is seamless and changeless.

The bodhisattva path is workable because it is not our limited self, ego, or personal sense of self and its accompanying psychological structure that is going to accomplish liberating ourselves and all beings. The meditations in which we cultivate compassion and love — in which we open into taking others' needs to be as important as our own — open us to experiencing who we are beyond our ego identity, beyond our ego operating system. These meditations update and upgrade our wiring, aligning us with our true nature. On my spiritual journey, there have been periods of time when I felt like I was being rewired. This is not always an easy process, but it has

107

---

* This phrase is a translation of a Tibetan and Sanskrit term that refers to the one flavor, the ultimate truth that pervades everything.

left me with an ego more transparent to pure being. Some of my walls have been taken down. This has led to deeper realization. In the eighties and nineties, I thought this rewiring was metaphorical. Scientific research has now proved that in fact this is true.[15]

Beyond self-interest, and the fact that being kind to others brings us happiness, loving-kindness is in alignment with who we truly are. Realization does not happen without it. Liberation cannot occur with a closed heart. Usually our hearts close, to varying degrees, because at some point we were so hurt that it was easier to shut down. These layers of defense against our pain may seem to work for a while, but it's an illusion.

COMPLETE MEDITATION
Step 3: Cultivating Awakened Mind

Set the feeling and intention that you are not just engaging in this meditation for yourself, but rather on behalf of, and for the benefit of, all sentient beings. Consider the suffering that all beings experience and the fact that awakening is what sets beings free and brings them lasting happiness and peace. Make your intention of awakening to benefit others and help lead them to genuine freedom, joy, and peace.

Then chant this prayer (which is also chanted in step 2):

> *Until awakening I take refuge in the Buddha,*
> *   the Dharma, and the Noble Sangha,*
> *By the merit of my acts of generosity and other*
> *   awakening qualities,*
> *May I attain full awakening for the benefit of all beings.*

Or chant the following prayer:

> *Just as the buddhas of the past aroused their altruistic awakened mind and applied themselves step-by-step to the training of a bodhisattva, so, too, in order to serve beings, I arouse my bodhicitta motivation and will pursue the training step-by-step.*

ON-THE-SPOT MEDITATION
Step 3: Cultivating Awakened Mind

This meditation can be used whenever you feel a need or desire to generate altruism or compassion, or want to offer your activities to a larger purpose. For example, I do it when I'm reading or hearing the news and thinking about the plight of refugees. Or, before starting work, you can pray, "May my work benefit many people." You can use this practice to reaffirm your values and goals. You can use it to align yourself as a vehicle to serve the greater whole.

Cultivate the wish to fully awaken in order to completely free others and yourself from suffering and to establish everyone in complete freedom, joy, and peace.

STEP 4

Stepping into Love

III

Your task is not to seek for love, but merely to seek and find all the barriers within yourself that you have built against it.

— RUMI

*T*he day that His Holiness the Dalai Lama won the 1989 Nobel Peace Prize, I attended his previously scheduled public talk on compassion at UC Irvine in Southern California. Thousands of us sat in the sports arena's steep rows looking down at him sitting simply on the stage. The Dalai Lama spoke about how he had worked for thirty-five years to resolve his anger, in particular his anger at members of the Chinese government, and how he had finally come to a place of compassion for them. He told us that for many years, he would get very upset when speaking with Chinese officials on the phone. He went on to say that eventually, after he had thoroughly transformed his anger, he would no longer get upset when speaking with them. Chuckling, he said that then they were upset that they couldn't get to him in the same way! His story demonstrates that even for an exemplary individual, it is hard work to fully liberate one's anger. It takes time. His effort demonstrates the power and efficacy of meditation and inner work to help us move past our suffering.

We are aware of so much suffering in the world: wars, terrorists, mass shootings, displaced refugees, American police killing innocents, and people being hurt or killed in so many ways. You may have suffered trauma yourself. It is healing to have a way to work internally with this sorrow in concert with the ways we are called on to work in the world. We can engage in the Love on Every Breath meditation in order to transform our relationship with suffering. We can turn discomfort, pain, and sorrow into compassion, love, and awakening. Our kindness and care for other beings, our world, and ourselves can increasingly open into unlimited love and compassion. We can turn feelings of powerlessness into being empowered by our Love on Every Breath meditation.

Vajrayana Buddhism uses our dualistic way of experiencing ourselves and our world as a stepping-stone to move into awakened presence and nonduality. This is part of the Love on Every Breath meditation. It is hard for us to open to our awakened nature, so a Vajrayana technique is to call upon an enlightened being, like Chenrezig or Tara, the female Buddha, and open to their presence. This allows us to connect with awakened mind and body. We can feel this because we have this nature within. In the meditation, we contemplate their qualities of wisdom and love.

We contemplate their other unique enlightened qualities as well. For example, with Tara, the ability to transform anxiety and fear into all-accomplishing wisdom. We call upon

Tara to transform and liberate our fear, and eventually we are able to transform our fears by ourselves. The enlightened being's body is seen as the union of luminosity, clarity, and emptiness, rather than a flesh-and-blood body. This helps us get in touch with the true nature of our body.

Meditating in this way creates a pathway for us to get in touch with awakened mind, presence, body, and speech inside ourselves, in our stream of being. Additionally, various methods are used in order to transform and liberate habit patterns, identity issues, and karma in general, to bring us into contact with, and eventually into, embodying complete awakening.

The following transformational meditation, Stepping into Love, helps us shift out of ego consciousness — shifting our identification from our conditioned, limited, and personal self to identification with pure being: the union of wisdom and love, our boundless awakened potential. Our innate awakened nature — unlike our personal self — has no trouble feeling others' suffering and transforming it into healing love.

113

Practicing Stepping into Love

The complete version of step 4 might seem complicated for those new to this kind of meditation. If so, feel free to use the On-the-Spot version.

To begin, imagine a bright lotus floating about a foot's distance straight above your head. On top of the lotus rests a flat disk of the moon. The lotus symbolizes that the pristine flowering of pure being can come out of the mud of our confusion and suffering. The moon stands for cooling, soothing altruistic compassion. The lotus and moon together symbolize the inseparability of the wisdom of realizing emptiness and the skillfulness of compassion.

Next, imagine that the Bodhisattva of Compassion, Chenrezig, comes to sit on the lotus moon seat cushion above your head. His body is made of white light and radiates rainbow light. Imagine him as clearly as possible. Over time as your meditation stabilizes, the clarity and luminosity of your visualization will become increasingly vivid. The most important point is to feel the awakened presence. As a reference, turn to the line drawing of Chenrezig on page 12.

Chenrezig's brilliant white body represents the luminosity of primordial wisdom, the spark of enlightenment. Five-colored light radiates from his heart. Half his hair is bound up, representing complete awakening, and half his hair is streaming down, indicating that he stays in *samsara* to benefit beings. He is sitting in vajra posture, the Buddhist term for sitting in the full lotus posture, symbolizing that he is awakened. If you have a spiritual teacher, think that Chenrezig is inseparable from him or her. In any case, think that he is the union of all awakened beings' love and compassion.

He holds a wish-fulfilling jewel in his two hands, which are in prayer position, or *mudra*, at his heart. The jewel symbolizes each person's innate awakened mind. Another hand holds a crystal mala,* or string of beads, signifying boundless compassionate activity of benefiting beings. As he recites the mantra of compassion, "*Om mani padme hum*" (pronounced "om ma-nee pad-may hum"), he moves one bead with each repetition of the mantra and draws the beads toward himself, symbolizing pulling beings out of suffering. Another hand holds the stem of a lotus flower, which symbolizes the

---

* A mala is a Buddhist or Hindu string of beads, similar to a rosary. It is usually made of 108 beads and is used to recite mantras.

enlightenment possible for each of us. Just as the lotus grows out of the muddy water, yet is pristine and gorgeous, so each of us has the potential to fully awaken in spite of our negative patterns and conditioning. It also symbolizes that Chenrezig is unstained by any faults and embodies the qualities of a Buddha.

He wears a crown set with five jewels of different colors. The white gem signifies the transformation of delusion into all-encompassing wisdom; the blue gem, that anger and aggression have transformed into mirror-like wisdom; the yellow jewel, that pride has become the wisdom of equality; the red gem, that desire and grasping have transformed into discerning wisdom; and the green jewel signifies that jealousy and fear have transformed into the wisdom of all-accomplishing activity. These wisdoms are natural energies within us, which, due to the patterns of our fundamental ignorance, often manifest in unwholesome ways. Chenrezig is also arrayed in other jewelry, signifying his accomplishment of the transcendent perfections. Rainbow silks clothe him. An antelope skin, signifying his loving nature, is around his shoulders.

On the highest point of Chenrezig's topknot is his guru, Amitabha Buddha, also known as the Buddha of Infinite Light. He is the Buddha of the Desire Realm, which is said in Buddhism to be the realm we reside in. He is ruby red in color, again symbolizing the transformation of desire into discerning wisdom.

As you meditate on Chenrezig above your head, from time to time contemplate the symbolic meaning of his form, his seat, and his implements. Imagine his eyes of wisdom gazing at you and all beings with unconditional love, the way a mother looks at her only child. Visualize all beings, infinite in number, surrounding you. Chenrezig is gazing upon all of them with this same love. Meditate on his vast compassion and vast love. Absorb this unconditional love.

Continuing to imagine Chenrezig above your head, pray to him as the union of all awakened love and compassion. In your own words, pray for the blessing of awakened love to flow into you and for your wisdom, love, and compassion to be fully activated. Pray that you may be of genuine lasting benefit to all beings and yourself. Pray that profound compassion and love for others and yourself awaken in your being and that it may grow ever stronger in your mind stream. The prayers help activate your innate empathy and love.

Through your prayers, Chenrezig dissolves into light and dissolves into you — you become Chenrezig with a body made of white light, radiating five colors. Your body, speech, and mind are inseparable from Chenrezig's awakened body, speech, and mind. Imagining yourself like this, visualize that you are seated on a lotus and moon seat. Your first two hands are in prayer *mudra* with a jewel held between them. The second two hold the lotus flower and crystal mala. You are arrayed in silks and jewels with the crown of the five Buddha families on your head. On your topknot is the Buddha of Infinite Light, Amitabha.

Then imagine a crystal vajra in your heart chakra (see page 13). This crystal vajra is luminosity, clarity, and emptiness inseparable. It represents and embodies the indestructible, birthless, and deathless essence of your awakened mind, the enlightened mind of your teachers, the buddhas and bodhisattvas, the saints and sages of all times and all places. It is capable of transforming your own and others' suffering into love and healing energy.

If you wish, you can expand this visualization to include Chenrezig. Imagine that in your heart chakra there is a tiny lotus and moon seat, and sitting within this is an extremely brilliant and radiant, tiny Chenrezig, who has the crystal vajra within his own heart chakra. This is the full visualization used in the traditional meditation, but simply imagining the crystal vajra is less complicated and often preferred. When you are new to this kind of meditation, these visualizations usually do not feel real, but over time, as you continue with the meditation, they will feel more and more real.

Continue to engage in this visualization, focusing primarily on the crystal vajra radiating love and healing energy as rainbow light to all beings. Occasionally look with your awareness at yourself as Chenrezig from different angles. Then, if you wish, either out loud or silently, chant the mantra "*Om mani padme hum,*" opening into love and compassion. This is the mantra of compassion, the mantra of loving-kindness, the Bodhisattva of Compassion Chenrezig's mantra. It translates roughly as "Om, the jewel in the lotus, hum." *Om* refers to awakened body, speech, and mind. According to the Dalai Lama, in this mantra, the jewel refers to altruism, the lotus refers to wisdom, and *hum* is the union of altruism and wisdom, which is the means of transforming our impure body, speech, and mind into liberated body, speech, and mind.

How long you chant the mantra is up to you. A significant number of repetitions includes 3, 7, 21, or 108 times, or multiples of 108. Traditionally, these numbers are considered auspicious. Usually you use a mala to keep track, moving one bead for each repetition of the mantra. It is said that the connection of the brain, hand, and speech helps anchor concentration, which eventually develops into *samadhi.**

As you chant the mantra, generate love for yourself and

---

* *Samadhi* is a Sanskrit term that means "a state of intense concentration." There are many kinds of *samadhi*, both in Hinduism and Buddhism.

all beings. Radiate the love out as light. Stabilize the sense of yourself as Chenrezig. Allow yourself to feel that you are one with all the love and compassion of all the buddhas and awakened beings. The feeling of awakened love inside of you will grow over time.

Then, reflect on your own and others' trials and tribulations and generate compassion for the suffering that you and others experience. Open to love and compassion, which are the heart of awareness. The mantra is the union of sound and emptiness, love and emptiness. As you say the mantra, imagine yourself as Chenrezig with a body of light, and the crystal vajra in your heart chakra becoming more and more brilliant, radiating the essence of empathy, love, and wisdom. Radiate from the vajra in your heart chakra love and kindness as brilliant rainbow light into your ordinary self and into others who are suffering.

The Importance of Chenrezig and the Power of Mantra

We usually work with the Bodhisattva of Compassion as a mentor figure in this meditation. In Tibetan, this figure is known as Chenrezig; in Sanskrit as Avalokitesvara. In both languages, his name means "The One Who Beholds with Loving Eyes." In Tibet, Chenrezig has several forms, all male, and the form that is taught traditionally with this meditation is that of a male, white in color, who has four arms. However, this being changed forms and gender in other cultures, becoming the female Quan Yin in China and the male Kannon in Japan. It is wonderful to use Quan Yin, or Tara, if you prefer a female.

Chenrezig is the embodiment of the enlightened compassion of all buddhas, of all enlightened beings, and of all our teachers. The story goes that Chenrezig has been working for eons to benefit beings. Whether one believes this or not does not matter. When we have realized awakened love and compassion, our mind is Chenrezig.

Love on Every Breath is a meditation that ultimately connects you to your true nature. Ultimately, it is pure indestructible stainless being, awareness itself, the union of luminosity, clarity, and emptiness, that does the work of healing. The meditation leads directly into this experience.

Further, chanting mantra is an important part of this meditation, since the sounds are a powerful means for expressing love, and the sounds themselves open the channels in our subtle bodies. Years ago, Stephen Levine, who was famous for his work in the field of death and dying, told a story about this. A person passing a bad accident on the freeway saw someone on a stretcher and immediately started praying for them and chanting the mantra "*Om mani padme hum.*" A year or two later, this person was very startled to receive a letter profusely thanking them for their prayers that day. The victim had almost died, but lying on the stretcher, she felt love being sent to her, heard the prayers and mantras from this random person driving by, and found it incredibly helpful. So she memorized the license plate number as the car passed, and when she recovered, she used the number to find the well-wisher and thank them.

Issues That Can Arise in Stepping into Love

At this stage, various forms of psychological resistance can come up, often around issues of authority and trust. Many people have been hurt or traumatized in the past by their parents, priests, or teachers. This is why Chenrezig is usually invoked instead of a human teacher. However, you might not want to open to a spiritual being outside yourself. One student of mine simply could not open to the idea of a buddha or bodhisattva being present within. Then when he reached step 5 (described next), he became overwhelmed by taking and sending and was blocked by psychological issues relating to his parents. He had to spend time working through these feelings before he could proceed.

Sometimes we feel deficient or unworthy and have to work through these feelings before we can open to the idea that an awakened being would help us. One of my friends told me years after the fact that he felt this way around Kalu Rinpoche. Rinpoche was very kind to him, but my friend always felt unworthy and deficient, so he did not take advantage of everything Rinpoche offered him. After Rinpoche had passed away, my friend regretted that he had missed some precious opportunities.

Some people feel that awakened beings don't exist, or that sages, saints, and awakened humans don't exist past death. I have discussed this earlier. If you feel this strongly, you may want to use a mentor who is still alive for this step.

Another common issue is to think: *It's too strange to meditate on this weird figure above my head, and even weirder to have him dissolve into me. What's the point?* The point is to help us shift from ego consciousness into feeling awakened energy, and then into awakened awareness. Through the centuries, thousands of yogis and yoginis in India, Nepal, Tibet, Mongolia, Bhutan, and Sikkim have found this to be efficacious. Now people all over the world find the same. Simply become the awakened one without any grandiosity or inflation. Don't overthink it; just be open and let it happen. Over time it will become increasingly real.

COMPLETE MEDITATION
Step 4: Stepping into Love

Call upon and imagine Chenrezig above your head. Aspire and pray to fully embody love and compassion for yourself and all beings and serve as a vehicle for healing.

In answer to your heartfelt aspirations, Chenrezig dissolves into light and into you. Feel that you are now inseparable from awakened body, speech, and mind, and especially from the love of the Bodhisattva of Compassion, who embodies the love of all the buddhas and bodhisattvas. You then appear in the form of Chenrezig, a body of light.

Inside your heart chakra is a crystal vajra of light — the essence of indestructible pure being, awakened love. If you wish, expand this visualization to include a small Chenrezig sitting on a lotus and moon seat in your heart, and inside Chenrezig's heart is the crystal vajra of light. Contemplate the suffering of all beings, and engender compassion for everyone, including yourself.

From the vajra, radiate love in the form of five-colored light to all beings and to your ordinary self. If you wish, chant, out loud or silently, the powerful mantra "*Om mani padme hum.*" Chant as long as you like, but traditionally in Buddhism, chanting 3, 7, 21, or 108 times is considered auspicious.

ON-THE-SPOT MEDITATION
Step 4: Stepping into Love

Use this On-the-Spot version whenever you feel an urgent need for help from the awakened beings, from the buddhas and bodhisattvas, from your lineage masters, or from your "higher power." For example, use it to help generate love and compassion if you are fighting with your spouse or partner, if you see a dead animal on the road, or if you see a parent speaking to their child harshly. I often do this step when I read the news and think of everything going on in our human world.

Feel that you are inseparable from awakened compassion and love, and appear as Chenrezig.

A crystal vajra of light in your heart radiates love as light out to one being, several, or all beings. Or simply see yourself in your ordinary form, filled with blessing and love.

Simultaneously, if you like, chant the mantra of compassion and love, "*Om mani padme hum.*"

The Heart of Love on Every Breath

Taking and Sending for Yourself

Compassion isn't some kind of self-improvement project or ideal that we're trying to live up to. Having compassion starts and ends with having compassion for all those unwanted parts of ourselves, all those imperfections that we don't even want to look at.

— PEMA CHÖDRÖN

*W*e have arrived at the Taking and Sending steps, which are the essence and heart of the Love on Every Breath meditation. Taking and Sending has two parts: Step 5 focuses on yourself, and step 6 focuses on others. Both are essential. In the first part (in this step), you contemplate the suffering of your ordinary human self, transform that with awareness and love, and send it back into yourself. In the second part (in step 6), you contemplate the suffering of other people, transform that with awareness and love, and send that back to them. Taking and Sending can be done in an instant, wherever and whenever you want, as a quick, in-the-moment response or as a full meditation on the cushion. If your heart feels closed down and you want to allow it to open, or you are in pain, you can do this meditation. As an ongoing daily or frequent meditation practice, it will transform your experience of yourself and others. Your heart will open and you will be connected to pure being.

What Is Love?

The love that I am describing in this book is a natural quality of our being. It is the love that springs from our true heart, reflected in our speech and actions. The ancient Greeks defined seven different states of love:

Storge: Natural affection, as in the love of a parent for a child.

Philia: Friendship love. This can be between friends or family members, and it represents sincere, platonic love.

Eros: Passionate love, both for a lover and for art, music, and beauty. This can also be passion for ideals, such as equality, freedom, and justice.

Agape: Unconditional love.

Ludus: Playful love, like childish love or flirting.

Pragma: Enduring love.

Philautia: The love of the self. The negative side of this is associated with narcissism and self-obsession; only seeking personal fame and fortune. The positive side is feeling good about ourselves, feeling secure, having self-esteem and confidence, and thereby having plenty of love to give others.

The love we are cultivating in Love on Every Breath is unconditional love, or agape. Yet it also includes every other type of love, except perhaps ludus. The meditation even includes eros if we include passion for ideals, since Love on Every Breath has passion for the welfare of all beings. Love eases our journey, making it more livable. It soothes our pain, lifts our heart, and brings forth our joy. Bringing awareness and love to our suffering is healing. In step 5 of Love on Every Breath, we cultivate compassion and love for ourselves.

Developing Self-Love

When I was in my early twenties, as I was walking out the door at the end of a therapy session, my therapist once asked, "What about self-love?" In the weeks and months that followed, I pondered this question, which helped me see my critical, judging mind. It had a lot of opinions that it freely shared with me. Again and again, while letting go of these critical thoughts, I tried to imagine what self-love would feel like. I kept working on letting self-critical thoughts go, feeling my way into loving myself. This went on for several years. One day, when I was twenty-six, I was studying and meditating in the Himalayan mountains in Darjeeling, India, at a Tibetan monastery filled with monks who were refugees. We had just finished a Dharma study class and walked out of a tiny retreat temple that was temporarily serving as a classroom. In the dim, late-afternoon light, Bokar Rinpoche, the heart disciple of my primary teacher, followed us out. He simply looked at me, and I felt and saw a lightning bolt of awakened love come from his heart into mine. Instantaneously, all my years of working on self-love came together with his awakened love. A profound shift took place inside of me. Self-love connected and became real in my heart. I have felt the balm of loving-kindness ever since in my dealings with myself. Since that moment long ago, this has made a huge difference in my life.

For instance, the ability to be gentle and loving with myself was incredibly helpful during the three-year meditation retreat that I began at the age of thirty. There was no way I was going to come up to the level of diligence, discipline, and enthusiasm that my teacher, Kalu Rinpoche, and the earlier lineage masters, like Milarepa, displayed in their long retreats, so having loving-kindness for myself allowed me to do the best I could and not beat myself up for not being or doing better.

Step 5, Taking and Sending for Yourself, is recommended in the oral tradition of the Shangpa lineage and also in the writings of one of the Shangpa lineage masters, Jamgon Kongtrul Lodro Thaye, the great nineteenth-century guru. The oral lineage advice that I received from my teacher, Kalu Rinpoche, the primary holder of this lineage, is that we do step 5 for several months before moving on to step 6, Taking and Sending for Others. That is, if we are doing the complete meditation daily, we do steps 1 through 5, skip step 6, and finish with steps 7 and 8. You might consider doing this yourself, if you plan to meditate daily or frequently, but if you only do the complete version of the Love on Every Breath meditation occasionally, I suggest you include all the steps every time, including step 6.

Ultimately, it is awareness itself, intrinsic to our being, that heals us. Support and kindness from others provide invaluable healing for us, but ultimately the healing takes place through our awareness. Transforming discomfort and suffering into love and compassion for ourselves, and working through the issues that arise in relation to this, is vital in the journey of the heart. No one is left out of a compassionate heart, even ourselves! Oftentimes we focus on others and don't consider ourselves. The human self goes through much hardship. This needs to be acknowledged and worked with. If we start at home, so to speak, with ourselves, opening to our pain, allowing it to be transformed and liberated into well-being, then not only are we healed, but we also have a capacity to be there for others. If we avoid our own pain, then it's hard to be fully empathic with others. Rather, we may try to "fix" others, or fix what's painful, which can be a way of avoiding our discomfort at others' distress. As Aristotle wrote, "All friendly feelings for others are an extension of a man's feelings for himself."

Practicing Taking and Sending for Yourself

To begin, imagine yourself as Chenrezig, visualize the crystal vajra in your heart center emanating brilliant light, and chant the mantra "*Om mani padme hum*" as many times as you like. If you are doing the full meditation, this is what you will have done in step 4, but if you are practicing this step separately, you can visualize this more quickly without necessarily doing all of step 4. The traditional instruction is to "flash on yourself as Chenrezig." Either way, this visualization is important preparation for step 5, as it helps us to open to and stabilize our sense of self as awakened presence, inseparable from the Bodhisattva of Compassion.

Once you've done this, imagine your ordinary self sitting in front of you. Reflect on and open to feeling the suffering of your human experience. Start with less intense feelings, and gradually over a few, or many, meditation sessions work up to more difficult feelings. Contemplate any sorrow, hardships, heartaches, and so on that you experience in your life, whether it be emotional, physical, mental, or spiritual. Open to feel natural compassion and love, just like you would for someone you love dearly. Gradually reflect further on all the challenges, disappointments, hurts, trauma, and so forth that you have gone through. If you get stuck and have a hard time feeling loving-kindness for yourself, don't worry. Don't berate yourself. Simply feel your pain to the extent that you can and proceed with the meditation. Either restabilize your consciousness in loving-kindness and continue, or include others who experience the same kind of suffering, and with loving-kindness and compassion, consider all your pain to-gether (see below). Indeed, if at any time during steps 5 and 6 you feel raw, vulnerable, and defenseless, or you feel a piercing sadness to the extent that it becomes hard to carry on with the meditation, refocus on yourself as Chenrezig for however long you like, whether it be a few moments or much longer. It may be for the whole meditation session. You can also chant the mantra of compassion, "*Om mani padme hum*," as many times as you like. This helps to stabilize your consciousness in loving-kindness and move your identification from being the one who is hurting to the one who is loving and healing. Then, when you are ready, continue with the meditation.

Further, as you contemplate your suffering in this medi-tation, another valuable way to work with it is to consider all the other people who are suffering with the same kind of pain or trauma. For example, if you are in trauma and pain after losing your home to a flood, you can think: *Oh, just like me, many people have lost their home. By my suffering this calamity, may all those suffering from the loss of their home be freed from this pain.* When we feel that we are not alone in our pain, it widens our view and puts our suffering in perspective. We can let go of fixating on ourselves and generate compassion and love for others. This produces a powerful internal shift from self-fixation to a larger awareness. It shifts us from a victim mentality to one of love, compassion, and increased equanimity. Then we can bring the empathy and loving-kindness back to ourselves.

As you continue with this meditation, open as much as you can to any sorrow or difficult feelings that come up. Feel great compassion and love for yourself. Contemplate the natural goodness in yourself. Again, at first it may prove challenging to feel loving-kindness for yourself, but if you stay with it over time, it will become easier.

Then synchronize the next visualization with your breath. On the in-breath, imagine the hurt or painful feelings as dark smoke that flows right into the vajra in your heart center. Instantly, the vajra, awakened mind, emits a white lightning bolt that completely transforms the suffering into awakened love and healing energy, which then appears as white light. It is not our ego self that does the transforming; rather, the vajra does it spontaneously. Then, on the out-breath, imagine the white light going back into your ordinary self sitting in front of you. Keep doing to this, repeating the visualization (and restabilizing as Chenrezig as necessary), until gradually you see your human self healed, filled with love, illuminated with white light, and awakened.

When this is complete, or when you feel ready to move on, rest with this for a few moments. At first, it may be challenging to align your breath with the visualization and your feeling of what is happening. If this is the case, don't worry. These will synchronize more smoothly as you become more familiar with the meditation.

A Mother's Grief:
The Healing Nature of Shared Suffering

Years ago, my friend Elena lost her four-year-old child to cancer. Devastated, she described walking the hospital corridors. Suddenly she realized that so many other parents had also lost a child, and her heart flooded with compassion and love for all of them. Her grief became part of the grief of all humanity, easing her own pain. Empathy arose in her spontaneously when she opened beyond herself to all the other parents who had also lost a child.

There is a famous story from the Buddhist scriptures about this. A mother came to the Buddha in complete despair, weeping, carrying the body of her dead baby, asking Shakyamuni Buddha to resuscitate her baby. He told her, "There is only one cure for this. You must bring me four or five mustard seeds from a family who has not had a death." The young mother immediately set out to find such a family. But in every household she visited, the family had had a death. Her grief lightened as compassion for the suffering of others naturally arose. She realized that suffering and death is inherent in life and that the death of a loved one happens to all of us at some time or another. Her excruciating grief lifted, and she was able to feel her sorrow within a larger context. She took the body of her child home to be cremated. Later, she became a disciple of the Buddha.

Ironically, when we let go of intense self-focus, as my friend Elena discovered, we can have increased empathy and love for ourselves as well. Self-absorption is not a loving state. It's a state of consciousness where one fixates on fulfilling our ego's self-interest. This does not transform suffering in the long run, as it simply concretizes the ego. This initial focus on loving the self is often the most challenging aspect of the entire meditation. We have a hard time with extending love to ourselves! We feel unworthy of love or unworthy of our caring attention. Each of us is a precious being. Each of us is fully worthy of love and healing. Subconscious fear of our pain can overwhelm us. Thomas Merton said, "The more you try to avoid suffering, the more you suffer, because smaller and more insignificant things begin to torture you, in proportion to your fear of being hurt. The one who does the most to avoid suffering is, in the end, the one who suffers most." This meditation is an opportunity to heal our wounds, to bring loving-kindness to ourselves, and to enhance our capacity to receive and give love.

If we override our pain and suffering, we end up shying away from others' suffering as well, trying to fix it instead of allowing and meeting it. If we wallow in our misery, or stay in a victim mentality, this is just another way to avoid facing our pain. It does not work, as it does not transform or liberate our suffering. If we are attached to being a victim or we are attached to our identity as "the one who suffers," our attention is on our false identity as an injured or hurt one, not on feeling the emotions themselves. This does not help, but often leads into a downward spiral. At this point, as the Buddha counseled, it is helpful to consider others who are having similar suffering, which is why this is part of step 5. The path of awakening requires kindness and gentleness with ourselves, and courage for being with and facing our pain. Getting support from others, from a therapist or another professional, can be helpful. Conscious allowing and facing of our suffering is what allows it to be transformed and liberated. When we gather the courage needed to face our pain, we have an increased capacity to be there for ourselves and for others.

Issues That Can Arise
in Taking and Sending for Yourself

Consider how every being is in their fundamental nature worthy and equally deserving of love. Consider how you love people dear to you, and how just like them, you are worthy of love, kindness, and compassion. Consider how all of us as human beings have flaws and imperfections, have learning and growing to do, and are nevertheless valuable, just as we are. We are unique beings, each with our special gifts.

We often find that it is difficult to allow ourselves to receive genuine love, from others or from ourselves. For many of us, it is easier to give love to others than to receive. Subconsciously or consciously, we feel that being stoic and strong will serve us best. In this meditation, if we notice our defenses arise against allowing love in, we can gently soften them so we can open to receive.

Once, long ago, I had an experience that highlighted this. In my late twenties, at the beginning of a six-week stay in Sikkim to see Karmapa, I came down with pneumonia. I was staying with a Tibetan family in their home just outside the monastery walls. I had my own room, which was a treat. They fed me simple, wholesome food. We could not speak each other's language, but they were kind. I indicated that I was doing fine, and they left me alone in bed. It was too far by curvy, potholed mountain roads, in an antique jeep, to even consider going to Gangtok, the capital and nearest town, for medical help. I just had to stay in bed until I was better. I wasn't worried that I didn't have medicine. It seemed like I would get better. My spirits were fine. At the time, I was married to Benchen Khenpo Rinpoche, a reincarnated Bhutanese lama. We were (and are) quite close, but he was busy in Bhutan at that moment.

However, there was no way to take a real bath or a shower, just a bucket, and even the toilet was a block away. So one day, after a month of pneumonia, I decided to go to the nearby home of Ashi Pema Dechan, the Bhutanese Queen Grandmother. At other times, when in Bhutan, I would take baths at one of her daughters' homes, so I thought it would be okay. I knocked at the door and was greeted by one of the princesses and her mother, Ashi Pema Dechen. When I saw them, they had so much compassion and kindness for me that I burst into tears while standing at the door. This greatly alarmed them, as Bhutanese and Tibetans very rarely, if ever, suddenly cry like that. Simply feeling their love burst my dam. They were so worried about me that they instantly went into action. I didn't even ask about taking a bath.

Unbeknownst to me, one of the Bhutanese princesses called my husband in Bhutan and told him to drive to Rumtek immediately. It was about a twelve-hour drive on the rugged, windy, narrow Himalayan roads. The drive was alarming. Trucks looked like they were coming straight at you and would pass within a couple of inches. Though I did not feel that I needed him to come, by the time I found out they had called, it was too late. I let in their loving care, but I was still too shy to ask them about a bath. My husband was with us by that same evening.

The next morning, with me still quite sick, Benchen Rinpoche took me to see His Holiness Karmapa. Karmapa said he hadn't known I was sick, and he kindly gave me some of his own personal Tibetan holy medicine from a pouch that he always wore around his neck. I took some of this medicine and amazingly, the next day I was almost all better. It is so healing, on many levels, to allow loving-kindness from others and from ourselves into our hearts. Thinking we have to keep a stiff upper lip usually just keeps our pain unprocessed, unmet, and buried until it finally raises its head and demands to be felt. The kindness and love we feel from others nourishes us in so many ways. It is invaluable in our lives.

Facing Pain, Discouragement, and Letting Go

Another issue that can arise during this meditation is fear of facing our pain and suffering. Indeed, if we cultivate compassion for ourselves, it can put us in direct contact with our emotions. It is so worth it! Having the courage to face our pain rewards us by lightening the load we carry. Everyone experiences pain and trauma, but the impact of traumatic experiences varies depending on the amount of help and support we receive. When traumatic things happen, the trauma is mitigated if, in the moment, we also receive support and compassion. However, experiencing love and support much later also helps in the healing process, whether that caring support comes from family, friends, or a professional.

134

In this meditation, overwhelm and discouragement can also arise. We may feel that our suffering is unworkable and permanent. We may think, *What's the use?* If you feel this way, it can be very helpful to simply let go of what you are doing in the moment and sit comfortably. Bring your attention into your abdomen and bring your breath there, too. Continue for some minutes, or for whatever time you have, to focus on and breathe into that area of your body, continuing to let go of everything else. This powerfully centers and anchors us in our life force energy. This meditation reminds me of those big plastic clowns that have ballast in the bottom. As much as you try to push the clown over, it keeps popping back up. When we are centered and grounded, we are like that, too.

Sometimes we are attached to our misery and don't really want to give it up. It may not be fun, but we are used to it. There is a certain familiarity to it. It may be a big part of us, and we might feel a scary, empty space if we let go. In the letting go process, we often feel our pain acutely as it comes up, right before it releases. When a wounding originally takes place, we do not usually have the resources to deal with what is happening, and so we repress it, shoving the pain away, or we split off from it. This is especially the case for children who do not have the resources to deal with the trauma or pain when it happens. And it happens for all of us. Unfortunately, the trauma doesn't leave. It is submerged, and we feel the tip of it. In life, in general, or in doing spiritual or psychological work, we may bring up our old pain in order to release it, flushing it out. At this point, when our misery comes to the surface, it carries with it all the original impact and intensity. This can feel quite intense, as though the wounding is happening all over again. This part of the process may take anywhere from a few minutes to days. It is important at this time to remember that our distress, discomfort, and pain is on its way out. In the words of Rumi:

> Sorrow prepares you for joy. It violently sweeps everything out of your house, so that new joy can find space to enter. It shakes the yellow leaves from the bough of your heart, so that fresh, green leaves can grow in their place. It pulls up the rotten roots, so that new roots hidden beneath have room to grow. Whatever sorrow shakes from your heart, far better things will take their place.[16]

As organisms, we shy away from facing our pain. However, this does not help us. Our discomfort and our unresolved distress surface again and again in a variety of ways. When our challenges and needs are not met with consciousness, we often act out in a variety of ways: We overeat, use drugs and alcohol, act out sexually; in short, we self-sabotage. Bringing love to meet our pain and discouragement is the ultimate medicine. The quality of our relationship to ourselves colors our entire life experience. This affiliation is twenty-four hours a day, seven days a week. Our neurotic patterns and our pain are workable. This is the gift of shunyata, of the emptiness of fixed identity. It is workable because it is not truly existent. We may not be able to completely liberate physical pain, but we can transform and liberate our relationship to it. We can transform and liberate our emotional and mental pain.

Nowadays, we have access to the great mystical traditions, in addition to modern psychotherapy. Both can be life changing. The spiritual path (and life itself!) often brings to the surface our psychological wounds and issues. At times on our spiritual journey, it can be helpful to do therapy to assist us in working these through. Our wounding almost always happens in the context of relationship, whether it is a one-on-one relationship, like that of a parent and child, or in a bigger context, like war. Working trauma or other issues through with another person, a skilled therapist, can be healing on the relational level. If you don't have the resources to do therapy, excellent self-help books abound. We have an amazing opportunity to let go, work through, release, and liberate ourselves in this lifetime! Loving ourselves eases the journey tremendously.

Ironically, it is our awareness, with its innate kindness and compassion, that in the end completes the job of healing and liberating us from suffering. Not only through profound realization, but through the simple act of bringing loving-awareness to meet our feelings and emotions. When we allow ourselves to open to our love, this is life changing. We have the opportunity with this meditation to do just that.

COMPLETE MEDITATION
Step 5: Taking and Sending for Yourself

To begin, imagine yourself as Chenrezig, enlightened being, the union of all awakened love and compassion, and in your heart chakra, imagine a vajra of crystal light that is the essence of awakened love and wisdom. If you like, you may see the vajra inside a tiny Chenrezig's heart. As many times as you wish, chant the mantra "*Om mani padme hum.*"

When this is done, imagine your ordinary human self sitting in front of and facing you.

Get in touch with any aspect of your suffering and open to loving-kindness and compassion for yourself. Work through any issues that arise, such as unworthiness. See your suffering as black smoke, and breathe it into your heart chakra. As soon as the smoke touches the vajra, let a lightning bolt of brilliant white light transform the suffering into awakened love, compassion, and healing energy. Breathe out this white light, awakened love, into yourself sitting in front of you. Repeat this process again and again, synchronizing the meditation with your breath. Imagine your ordinary self filling with white light, which is awakened love. This light alleviates suffering and brings about awakening. Imagine yourself becoming gradually healed, illuminated, and awakened.

Occasionally restabilize the sense of yourself as awakened presence, as the awakened Bodhisattva of Compassion inseparable from the presence, wisdom, and love of all the enlightened ones.

One option, if you wish, is to modify the meditation like this: After getting in touch with one aspect of your suffering, consider all the people who suffer with the same or a similar affliction. For example, think: *Oh, just like me, many people suffer from headaches! By my suffering this headache, may all those suffering from headaches be freed from this pain.* Then imagine all these people in front of you, surrounding your ordinary self. Imagine your own and everyone's suffering as black smoke, and imagine that your own and everyone's suffering, simultaneously and at once, is transformed by the vajra.

ON-THE-SPOT MEDITATION
Step 5: Taking and Sending for Yourself

Do this meditation whenever you want to generate loving-kindness for yourself; whenever you are having a hard time, are sick or in pain, are facing challenges, or are doing inner healing work; or for transformation and opening the heart. When I feel bad that I have repeated an unwholesome pattern, I resolve to be more mindful, and then I do this On-the-Spot version and feel in touch with loving-kindness.

Imagine your ordinary self in front of and facing you. Open into feeling any suffering that is present in your human self, and open to feel loving-kindness and compassion for yourself.

See your human self's suffering as black smoke, and breathe it into the vajra in your heart chakra. As soon as it touches the vajra, a lightning bolt emerges from the vajra, instantly transforming the suffering into white light that is awakened love and healing energy.

Breathe out the transformed energy as white light into your human self in front of you. See the white light filling your ordinary self, bringing healing and awakening. See yourself as healed, awakened.

Repeat this, for as long as you like, synchronizing the visualization with the breath.

One option, if you wish, is this modification: After contemplating your suffering, think about all those who are suffering in a similar way, and think, for example: *Oh, just like me, many people suffer from headaches! By my suffering this headache, may all those suffering from this be freed from this pain.* Then imagine all these people in front of you, surrounding your ordinary self, and do the Taking and Sending visualization for the whole group simultaneously with yourself.

The Heart of Love on Every Breath

Taking and Sending for Others

To live in love is to sail forever,
spreading seeds of joy and peace in hearts.

— ST. THÉRÈSE OF LISIEUX

Some years ago I was invited by an eclectic group of Buddhist meditators to teach a weeklong retreat in Four Corners, where Utah, Colorado, New Mexico, and Arizona meet. Arriving there with the sunlight illuminating the juniper trees and fragrant sage plants, I gazed up at the cliffs and remembered this was land that had belonged to the Anasazi, a Native American people. The cliffs were dotted with caves that had served an entire village hundreds of years earlier. In addition to the caves and the rooms carved into the cliffs, there was also an underground kiva, a place for the ancient ceremonies.

After we had been settled into meditation for five or six

days, I was guiding the Love on Every Breath meditation with the group. We were at least an hour into the meditation, nearing the conclusion, when all of a sudden, in my inner vision, a Native American chief appeared. He was walking toward me in the shrine room, which in the vision had no walls. There were about three hundred of his people behind him. This type of vision was an unusual occurrence for me, so I wondered what was going on. His presence was vivid, and it was obvious that he was coming to see me with a purpose. Silently, I asked him what he was doing there. He indicated that they were feeling the powerful love of the taking and sending, so they came. He told me that he and his people needed love and acknowledgment. In that moment, filled with care and respect for him and his people, I engaged in taking and sending for them. There wasn't a lot of time left in the session, but I did my best and promised them that I would work with them more later. Archaeologists don't know what wiped out the entire population there, but somehow this group was stuck and they really wanted and needed love. Later, in my own meditation, I did a long session of Love on Every Breath for them, and I continued to do so for some weeks.

Additionally, I realized that it would be good to do another meditation specifically for the native people of this place. The meditation I wanted to do, the Rio Sang Chöd (which I mention in step 3), comes from Padmasambhava, a great *mahasiddha** who was the primary force in bringing Buddhism to Tibet. During the meditation, we offer the smoke from burning cedar and juniper, and in North America, we often add sage. We offer the plant smoke to the awakened ones, to all saints and sages, and then to all beings — and particularly to the nature spirits. There was no time to do the meditation

---

*   *Mahasiddha* is Sanskrit for a greatly accomplished spiritual adept.

ceremony during this retreat, but I vowed to myself that I would do it for these spirit beings the following year.

The next year I was fortunate to return to the same land to lead another retreat. After I shared what I had seen the year before in my inner vision, we did the smoke-offering meditation together in the early-morning light. We engaged in the Love on Every Breath meditation for the tribe. Following this, it seemed that the tribal spirits were satisfied and at peace. They thanked me for the love they received. They communicated to me that it was love they had been craving and they felt fulfilled.

Love is the only thing that can meet the state of affairs of humankind, where power and greed seem to rule. Yet today, as well as throughout all times, there are people who care about others, people who care about the good of all — people who hold love in their hearts and help others. We have so many opportunities at this time to be part of changing things for the good for all. We are not powerless. We can affect the world. And we can definitely affect our mind. There are countless examples of human kindness, people working to make things better for others, and people who spontaneously reach out and help others, whether or not it is safe to do so. These people inspire us and open our hearts. We continually have an opportunity to promote and celebrate our human values of compassion, honesty, truth, equality, justice, freedom, and love. Opening our heart to others, learning to love others and care for them, brings us joy and peace, and opens us to our interconnectedness.[17] We can transform our experience of self, our experience of others, and our experience with all that is. The heart essence of this practice is to breathe into the pain, suffering, or discomfort we feel in our heart.

Then, with our wish to alleviate suffering, we allow the pain to be transformed into love and healing energy.

Transforming Suffering into Love and Joy

We take on so much sorrow, pain, and tragedy through everything we see, hear, and feel in our experience and through the media. This is like breathing in suffering. We do this subconsciously because we care about our fellow human beings, about animals, about our planet. But if this suffering sits inside of us, it just weighs us down, dampening our happiness and well-being. If we consciously acknowledge our experience of the suffering of the world, we can transform our inner experience. We can allow it to be transformed by the light of our true nature, our buddha nature.

The ever-present loving awareness and openness of the vajra, the essence of awakened presence, transforms the suffering. Love and compassion are process oriented. Love sounds like a thing that you have or don't have. But we can consciously grow our love. The Dalai Lama has said that in his daily meditation he cultivates loving-kindness and compassion. Pema Chödrön says, "By dissolving ego's barriers, compassion naturally arises."

Spiritual tools, like Love on Every Breath, can nourish, sustain, transform, and liberate our hearts. This can fuel and empower our work in the world. Whether or not we actively engage in the world, doing our meditation makes a difference — as we transform our consciousness, it changes and benefits the consciousness of the whole. If we are actively engaged with shifting things for the better, this meditation helps to sustain our love, caring, strength, equanimity, and groundedness in our deepest principles. It increases our happiness and sustains us.[18]

144

The primary purpose of the Love on Every Breath meditation is to develop and open to our innate love and compassion, to transform and liberate our heart, our true nature. When we come from a place of love, everything shifts for us. However, there are times and ways this meditation can change our relationships and change other people's experience as well. For example, when we are in distress about a relationship with a loved one, our Love on Every Breath meditation can help us move from an emotionally agitated and possibly defensive place to one of more openness and empathy. We move into more equanimity; we can feel their innate goodness and vulnerability. This allows more space and love to be present in the relationship. When we are not holding on to a fixed idea of another, and we have openness and empathy for them, it's remarkable how the other person will often show up in a different way.

When we are struggling with our suffering, we can turn it to awakening. We can consider all those who, like us, suffer from the same kinds of problems, circumstances, or challenges. We can bring all our suffering into our Love on Every Breath meditation. This opens our heart and changes our perspective.

The Naturally Occurring Power of Love

Years ago, Jetsunma Tenzin Palmo, an Englishwoman who has been a Vajrayana Buddhist nun since the early sixties, told me a story of a spontaneous prayer her mother made when a boiling pot overturned onto Jetsunma when she was a child. Instantly, upon witnessing this horrific scene, her mother prayed fervently, "May I feel all the pain instead of my daughter!" For months afterward, Jetsunma was in the

145

hospital being treated for burns. The doctors and nurses kept telling her what a wonderful, brave girl she was for never complaining about the pain or crying out when they changed the bandages. But Jetsunma said she wasn't being brave or stoic; she just didn't have any pain.

After many weeks of this, she wondered about it and thought to herself, *What would this pain really feel like?* Then she felt excruciating agony for five minutes before it disappeared. Later she spoke with her mom about this, and her mom shared how she had prayed. Her mom said she didn't feel any pain, either. This is obviously a very unusual occurrence, their personal experience of the power of love.

Practicing Taking and Sending for Others

After step 5, we are now ready to practice Taking and Sending for Others. Over the previous steps, we have let go and rested in sheer awareness. We have the support of the awakened refuge beings; we have engendered a strong sense of altruism, of wanting to be of benefit to others and ourselves; and we have prayed to be able to be vehicles of love, compassion, and healing. We have received the blessing of the awakened Bodhisattva of Compassion and become one with his body, speech, and mind. We have attended to our suffering and felt the healing power of awakened love.

In step 6, we work with one person, with two people, or with many. As a beginner, start with one or two, and gradually, over time, include more and more people in your meditation. Further, start with someone you really love and appreciate, whether the person is still alive or not. Traditionally, we start with our parents, since in Asia parents are revered and people feel grateful to them. However, in Western culture, we often feel a lot of conflict in regard to our parents. We may have been hurt or damaged by them. These things happen in the West, and they happen in Asia as well, but their cultural attitude is different. At any rate, if you have internal struggles with your parents, it is not helpful to start with them. In this case, choose someone else first, and work with your parents when you feel ready.

Begin by feeling yourself as inseparable from and appearing as Chenrezig. See and feel the vajra of crystal light in your heart chakra, per the instructions in step 4. Then imagine the beloved person, or persons, sitting or standing in front of you. Consider their challenges, traumas, distress, and adversities. Open to feeling compassion and loving-kindness for them. Contemplate the suffering they are going through or have gone through in the past. Even those who seem to have everything still suffer. Indeed, our first-world problems are superficial compared to the danger, abuse, and poverty that many live with. *But suffering of any kind is suffering.* The successful person who has accomplished all their career and personal goals may look like they have it all, and yet they may still feel unfulfilled, buffeted by neurotic thinking, or not at peace with themselves. We can see this if we look at the recent suicides of celebrities who seem to "have it all."

Reflecting that you would like to relieve their pain and bring them into the permanent and lasting happiness of awakening, breathe in their suffering as black smoke into your heart chakra. As before, as soon as the suffering touches the vajra, the vajra instantly emanates a lightning bolt that transforms the pain into white light, awakened love, compassion, and healing energy. Breathe this out to them. Keep breathing in the suffering as black smoke, see and feel it transform, then breathe out the white light, love, and transformed energy

147

into the person or people in front of you. Do this over and over, synchronized with your breath. During this process, you can consider the various sufferings they have had to endure. Imagine all their obscurations, conflicting emotions, mental misunderstandings, karma, and suffering liberated into wisdom love.

All suffering is impermanent, all obscurations are impermanent, and all conflicting emotions, such as anger, lust, pride, and jealousy, are impermanent. Phenomenon's essential nature is luminosity, clarity, and openness and can be transformed on an apparent level. On a genuine level it is already pure and liberated. All our problems, faults, hurt, and failings are not the unchanging nature of who we really are, so they can be transformed.

148 It is also beneficial to consider the love, friendship, and instances of kindness that the person you are working with has shown you. Reflect on how their kindness may have helped you in the past and how it may be helping you now. If their kindness opened doors for you, or helped you to take a new step, then contemplate that, too. Consider whether or not they were obligated to help you or did so simply from the goodness of their heart. Either way, you benefited. Feel the appreciation grow for the benefit you have received.

Gradually, see the person or people in front of you filled with light and awakened love. Imagine them healed, happy, illuminated, and awakened.

From time to time, focus on yourself, rest as Chenrezig, and clarify your heart chakra visualization. Focus on your body of light, feel your union with the awakened presence of the body, speech, and mind of the Bodhisattva of Compassion. Gradually focus on various details of your experience and reflect on the meaning of your symbolic form. Rest in the sense of yourself as an awakened being. Stabilize in this. Whenever you like during steps 5 and 6, repeat the mantra "*Om mani padme hum.*" When you are ready, go back to taking and sending. Look at the beings in front of you with eyes of great love, the heart overflowing with compassion. Drawing in all negativity and having the vajra explode suffering into awakened love, the light of the vajra becomes more and more illuminated, at ease, brilliant, with all its qualities manifesting.

As with any meditation, if your mind wanders, simply come back to the meditation without self-judgment. If your mind feels dull or sleepy, increase the brilliance of the vajra. This will increase clarity and wakefulness.

When you feel ready, after engaging in taking and sending with one or a few people for a period of time, you can move to the conclusion of the meditation session. Or visualize more people and continue with the full meditation as described below.

In the complete version of step 6, continue taking and sending with other loved ones and close friends, and then gradually expand to acquaintances, to colleagues, and eventually to all the people you know. Imagine all the people you have had contact with in your life even if you can't remember all of them. Imagine that they are all in front of you, facing you, and you are doing Tonglen for all of them as a group. Keep doing Taking and Sending for Others as long as you like, and see others filling with light, being healed, at peace and in joy, awakened.

As you proceed, you might focus on particular people, or a particular group, within the larger group, addressing them one at a time. As before, start with those for whom you naturally feel compassion, and wait to address those you have difficulties with. As you visualize each person or group, bring them to the forefront, while the people you've already worked with move to the sides. Do the taking and sending, gradually seeing others healed, illuminated, awakened. Examples of those you might feel natural compassion for include people suffering from illness or injury; those affected by war, terrorism, random violence, abuse, discrimination, and greedy policies; those in the hospital and in prison. Keep taking and sending until you come to the point where you imagine all of them free of suffering, healed, full of joy, and awakened.

Next, bring the difficult people to the front (see the next section for more advice on this). Open to feel their pain and confusion, seeing it as a dark smoke-like substance; breathe it into the vajra of brilliant light. Instantly see and feel the lightning bolt transform the suffering into white light, awakened energy. Imagine that this white light goes back into the person or people, healing them and liberating all their confusion. See them gradually awaken to the truth of cause and effect, to our interconnectedness as beings, to the nature of reality and of who they really are. See them being purified and filling with the luminous light of love and compassion. Imagine them gradually awakening.

Then widen your focus and imagine the whole of humanity, like a vast ocean of beings, in front of you. You may also include all the animals, if you like. Do Taking and Sending for Others for everyone as a group. Go through the same process of seeing their suffering transformed by the vajra and its lightning bolt; see them healed, illuminated, awakened. Eventually, look at this vast gathering of beings, all of them illuminated and enlightened. Rest in yourself as Chenrezig and in the peace and joy of all of us awakened together. Let yourself really open into this, really feel it. Being able to imagine this, and rest in it, helps carve a pathway for this to actually happen.

One variation of this meditation, which you can do at any time, is to think of all the people you've had contact with that day, and send all their energy back to them as the perfect healing light of awakened love. As I mention above, we often take in other people's energy without knowing it. If we take it in and it's not transformed, it gets stuck in our system and drags us down. It's not helping others and it's not helping us. It just sits inside of us, stagnating. We can't process other people's stuff. We can only process our side of the equation, and we each need to do our own work. I usually use a white or deep blue light in this process. So if we send everyone's energy back to them, as perfect healing light, we are refreshed and renewed. Now what we have on our plate is ours alone.

Sending people's energy back to them as healing is also very beneficial for us if we are in the helping professions. I have found this to be useful. We work with people and feel empathy for them, and we may subconsciously take on their problems, which again just sit in our systems. We can't process others' challenges for them. We can certainly be a tremendous support. We can assist with life-saving and life-changing interventions. We can counsel, go with people to appointments, bring food, and perform a myriad of other worthwhile tasks. But we cannot resolve their inner issues for them.

Additionally, anytime we're feeling overwhelmed, we can call upon Chenrezig to come into us and be present with us. A lot of us are empathic and care about the whole of humanity. We can get overwhelmed by what is going on in our world. We can gift others, in our small way, by working to stabilize a caring, loving, peaceful mind. This of course is mainly helpful for our development and awakening, but our drop in the bucket to help the whole can include actualizing awake, sane energy and then spreading the energy of compassion and love.

Working with People Who Are Difficult

When I despair, I remember that all through history the way of truth and love have always won. There have been tyrants and murderers, and for a time, they can seem invincible, but in the end, they always fall. Think of it — always.

— MAHATMA GANDHI

When you are ready, it's time to work with the people for whom you have difficulty feeling loving-kindness and compassion, whether because they have hurt you or others. Don't rush this step; if you are doing the meditation and want to skip certain people, it's best to do so for now, and at some later time work with them when your meditation is more established. The Love on Every Breath meditation is meant to be done regularly, many times, until you gradually include everyone.

Before addressing difficult people, remember to take the time to heal your wounds. This may include doing some (or more) psychotherapy to process any pain and anger before working on forgiveness and compassion within this meditation. Then, at this point during the meditation, you may want to do Taking and Sending for Yourself again. Don't try to forgive before you are actually ready in order to do the Love on Every Breath meditation for a challenging person.

When you are ready, start with the ones who are the least difficult. Once you have worked with them successfully, you can work with the more challenging people. Consider how the person's harmful actions are based on ignorance. If

people understood that we are all interconnected, like different parts of one body, they would not want to hurt or destroy
one part of the whole. Consider how sometimes people think
that their damaging behavior is going to bring them happiness. Maybe in a flash of anger someone thinks that blasting
their spouse or children with cutting remarks is a good idea
and will help them feel better. Maybe it seems that joining
a gang is someone's only alternative for being safe. Maybe
someone believes that surreptitiously attacking a coworker
while talking to the boss is the way to advance oneself. A man
might think hitting his wife is an okay thing to do because
his father, his uncles, and his grandfathers did it. One of my
friends works with perpetrators of domestic violence, and
the men have told her again and again that they thought violence was normal because of how their elders acted. They
break down crying when they find out how this hurts their
family and that there are alternatives for solving their problems. Maybe an elected official thinks lying to and betraying
constituents is okay if it furthers their own agenda. Maybe
a CEO or board director thinks that corporate policies that
harm people or the environment are not a problem if they
increase the bottom line. This is all great ignorance. We are
never going to achieve happiness by hurting others or by destroying our planetary home.

153

One of my friends, Sherry Anderson, wrote a book with
her husband, Paul Ray, many years ago called *The Cultural
Creatives*. As part of their research for the book, they inter-
viewed various people. My friend asked a CEO of a large
company, "How do you feel about how your company policies will affect your children and grandchildren's generation?" He replied, "I try never to think about that." Is this a

way to live that brings happiness? Yet his decision supported the destructive actions of his corporation.

Understanding that everyone wants happiness and is trying to be happy, we can understand that some people are confused about how to go about that. They harm others and think this will bring them happiness. We see this in the extreme with people who are violent. They think that this will bring them peace.

Negative and harmful actions never bring us happiness. If we don't believe the teachings on karma — of cause and effect, or as taught in the Bible, "Whatsoever a man soweth, that shall he also reap" — we can look to the research on what brings us happiness. We can see that when we engage in harmful or unskillful actions, this does not bring us happiness. We can see that people who harm others are not at peace; despite their bravado, they are miserable.

Research shows how compassion and anger affect us physically and psychologically in different ways.[19] In one study's participants, following experiences of anger and frustration, the heart rate increased and the level of immunoglobulin A, which is the immune system's first line of defense, decreased. After they experienced care and compassion, the opposite occurred. Contemplating this, we can begin to have compassion for people who act destructively. Without in any way condoning their actions, we can have compassion for them in their ignorance. When we do harmful things to ourselves or others, if we engage with the Love on Every Breath meditation thoroughly, we will retain compassion and lovingkindness for ourselves, as well as remorse and decisive intention to refrain in the future from those actions. This is a foundation for having compassion for others. When we are humble about how hard it is to change our negative patterns, we have more compassion for others. So, contemplating that people who cause harm to others are trying to achieve happiness, albeit selfishly, we can open to feeling compassion for them and wish for them to awaken from their ignorance. Research shows that giving to others brings us pleasure and happiness.[20]

In order to understand people who are destructive, we can also reflect on their upbringing and on other bases of their psychological makeup. Again, this is not to excuse their behavior, but rather to help us perceive what is going on with them and have compassion for their ignorance and suffering.

The Power of Love with Difficult People

As an example, I recently heard a news story about a fellow who wanted to have real discussions with people holding white supremacist views. He made contact with a few of the leaders of this movement on the East Coast. Over time, the man listened and also shared his thoughts and feelings without trying to ram his position down their throats. He got to know a few leaders and became friends with them. Eventually, several heads of regional chapters ended up changing their views and resigning, and some of the others he had become friends with also changed their perspective and dropped out of the white supremacist movement.

Along similar lines, one of my students had this to say after a meditation session I led for a group: "I learned this meditation from you some time ago, but hadn't done it in a while. I was really surprised at how it was energizing for me this time. Toward the end of the meditation, when we're working with people who do or did really bad things, I saw all the ISIS leaders, and then all of a sudden Osama bin Laden jumped in, as well as some other political leaders. It really felt like, from the depths of their being, they have a big need for healing love. I felt a lot of gratitude coming from them, which made it easier to continue."

Understanding that destructive, harmful people are cut off from their true nature can help us to have compassion for them. In spite of their terrible, twisted acts, they are redeemable, they are worthy of love, and they can transform. Given the circumstances that such people have grown up with, we might have ended up like them. If we look at ourselves clearly, we can see our own anger and greed, as in, "There but for the grace of God go I." Being willing to be honest with ourselves brings humility. It makes it easier for us to have compassion for others when we acknowledge how hard and slow it can be for us to change. Sometimes it is difficult to see any options. We can focus on how all of us do things out of the fundamental ignorance of who we truly are, and our patterns of mind and behavior can be very damaging. It doesn't mean that there should not be consequences for those who harm others, that we shouldn't, for example, put people in jail. But it is a recognition that we want transformation for these people, for the negative parts of ourselves, that we want actual healing. If all those who are destructive could awaken, that would be a good thing.

Transformation at San Quentin

As a further example, Susan Shannon, a close friend, is a Buddhist and interfaith chaplain at San Quentin, a state prison for men in the San Francisco Bay Area. San Quentin inmates have benefited over the years from spiritual and educational programs that chaplains and others have delivered.

However, before Susan, no one had ever been granted permission to do meditation groups for death-row prisoners. San Quentin's death row has more prisoners awaiting execution than any other prison in the United States. In addition to her regular meditation groups in the prison, Susan now has seven groups for death-row inmates. The groups she leads are not just meditation groups; they incorporate Buddhist teachings, such as teachings on generosity, ethics, patience, joyful exertion, concentration, and wisdom. They incorporate the teachings of love and compassion, of altruistic motivation. Susan's joyful discovery is that many of the men are transforming their entire outlook. They are transforming their hearts onto the path of love. They are making actual concrete changes in their behavior while in prison.

There is another Buddhist teaching that is pertinent here. In understanding our interdependence with all beings, with all that is, we can contemplate that all of what we experience is a reflection of our mind and karma. An excerpt from Thich Nhat Hanh's famous poem titled "Call Me by My True Names" addresses this eloquently.

157

> *I am the child in Uganda, all skin and bones,*
> *my legs as thin as bamboo sticks,*
> *and I am the arms merchant, selling deadly weapons*
> *to Uganda.*
>
> *I am the twelve-year-old girl, refugee on a small boat,*
> *who throws herself into the ocean after being raped by*
> *a sea pirate,*
> *and I am the pirate, my heart not yet capable of seeing*
> *and loving.*[21]

Most of us don't want to hurt people. Of course, we inadvertently hurt each other. Yet on the spiritual path, we eventually come to recognize that, like Thich Nhat Hanh's poem, everyone is interconnected. Everyone is a reflection of ourselves, whether it's Buddha, Jesus, the Dalai Lama, a murderer, a greedy person, or whoever. We can have compassion if we contemplate this — a human being backed into a corner again and again, who has an abundance of difficult circumstances, may take a turn onto a bad road. We can wish that they sincerely regret, reform, and are healed, that their buddha nature blossoms. We can pray that they are able to enter a path of peace and awakening.

Issues That Can Arise in Taking and Sending for Others

The primary issue that arises for people learning this meditation is the thought, *I'm already overwhelmed by suffering — my own and that of so many. The last thing I want is to feel more pain!* As I discuss in step 5, for us as human beings, the only way to fully alleviate our suffering is to feel it. It does not resolve when we ignore it, using our favorite strategy to keep it at bay. Some of our strategies are healthier than others, for example, being a workaholic is healthier than being an alcoholic. Nevertheless, we need to face what is present in us, with loving-kindness and compassion, and work it through in ourselves first. This is one of the reasons we become Chenrezig — to open into greater capacity. Then we will not be overwhelmed by others' pain.

There are two main paths that can work to liberate our suffering and bring us to true peace and happiness. They are not mutually exclusive, but rather they support and empower each other. The first way is through inner work, spiritual or psychological or both, in which we directly work with our pain, engaging in inner healing and transformation. This turns our misery into compassion, understanding, contentment, and happiness. The second way is, instead of floundering in our gloom, we focus on service for others. This helps alleviate our distress and sorrow and can increase our compassion, sense of meaning, fulfillment, and joy. Science is showing that giving to others brings us happiness.[22] However, this second path can also lead to burnout, a kind of martyrdom, which is physically and psychologically unhealthy. Service can also be a form of avoidance. In order to prevent this, we need to have a balanced lifestyle and learn how to nourish and sustain ourselves.

Love on Every Breath is valuable for both of these paths because it can process, transform, and completely liberate our suffering. The energy that has been trapped inside of us in a configuration of pain is then freed up as love and joy. I have had the experience many times of doing this Tonglen in a long sitting, and the amount of love that opens up is amazing. It feels like nothing else I've ever felt — tender yet strong, delicious, and joyful. The love fills my whole being, especially my heart chakra, exquisite in its radiance. This energy then directly feeds into all our activity in the world, both work and play, energizing our interactions with kindness, with love, with joy.

159

Another disconcerting thing that can arise while doing this part of Love on Every Breath is that your heart physically hurts. Occasionally, during the meditation, we can feel like there is a physical pain in our heart center. These are "growing pains," or tensions and blocks releasing. They come and go at different times. They vanish when we get up from the cushion, if not before. A well-known Buddhist teacher told a story years ago of a physician at a Vipassana retreat. He had so much pain in his heart chakra that he thought he was having a heart attack. But no, it was simply the subtle body letting go of old contractions. It passed and he was fine.

Boundaries are another issue that can arise while doing Taking and Sending for Others. Sometimes it is not so easy to discern what is ours to do and what is the other person's responsibility. This issue highlights why it is important for us to shift into being Chenrezig. Staying on our side of the fence becomes easier, and the appropriate boundaries for ourselves become clearer.

COMPLETE MEDITATION
Step 6: Taking and Sending for Others

To begin, imagine yourself as Chenrezig, enlightened being, the union of all awakened love and compassion, and in your heart chakra, imagine a vajra of crystal light that is the essence of awakened love and wisdom. If you like, visualize the vajra inside a tiny Chenrezig in your heart. As many times as you wish, chant the mantra "*Om mani padme hum.*"

When this is done, see the person or people in front of you whom you want to work with. Contemplate their suffering and open to feel loving-kindness and compassion for them.

Synchronize this visualization with your breath: On the in-breath, breathe in their suffering as black smoke, and see it instantaneously, spontaneously transformed by the lightning bolt emanating from the vajra. This transforms their suffering into white light, awakened compassion, love, and healing energy.

Breathe out this light into the person or people in front of you. Repeat this visualization until you see them filling with light, being healed, happy, and awakened.

Occasionally restabilize the sense of yourself as awakened presence, as the awakened Bodhisattva of Compassion inseparable from wisdom and love. If you like, repeat the mantra "*Om mani padme hum*" for a time.

Gradually extend your Love on Every Breath meditation to include all beings, imagining them in front of you. Finally, imagine everyone filled with white light, healed, liberated, and completely awakened. Rest in this.

ON-THE-SPOT MEDITATION
Step 6: Taking and Sending for Others

Do this version whenever you want to open your heart, or wish to give love, compassion, or healing energy to others. For example, it can be helpful to do this On-the-Spot meditation if a loved one is ill or distressed, if you witness suffering by anyone, if you want to send caring and love to a homeless person, if you pass a car accident and see injured people, or if you witness a coworker being treated badly. It can also be especially beneficial for healers, therapists, nurses, activists, and service providers, among others, to help them process what they take in daily and to prevent burnout. I often do this On-the-Spot meditation when I am in meetings or when I hear about a friend who's having a tough time. I've found that if I'm upset with someone, doing this meditation transforms my energy and my feelings. Similarly, if you are down, doing this meditation will lift your spirits and get your mind off yourself. I love doing this On-the-Spot.

Envision a crystal vajra of light in your heart. See the person or people in front of you whom you want to work with. Contemplate their suffering and open to feel loving-kindness and compassion for them.

Breathe in their suffering as black smoke, and see it instantaneously, spontaneously transformed by the lightning bolt emanating from the vajra. This transforms their suffering into white light, awakened compassion, love, and healing energy.

Breathe out this light to the person or people in front of you. See them filling with light, being healed, happy, and awakened.

For an even briefer version:
Breathe into suffering. See and feel it transformed by the crystal vajra and the lightning bolt of enlightened heart-mind. Breathe out love to yourself and all beings, to the entirety of what is.

Dissolving

There is nothing like returning to a place that remains unchanged
to find the ways in which you yourself have altered.

— NELSON MANDELA

Now we come to letting everything dissolve into vast sky-like openness and emptiness. We move from form to formlessness again. We let all the beings we have been envisioning dissolve into space, like a rainbow dissolves into the sky. We let our thoughts and feelings of loving-kindness dissolve into space. We let the crystal vajra of light, our form as the embodiment of enlightened love, dissolve into space.

Rest in the feeling that is present in the aftermath of this loving meditation. Rest in the love and the feeling of vastness. Let go of all thoughts, all conceptuality, all sense of a reference point, and let your awareness mix with space. Let go into peace. Anything that is still hanging on, let it go. Let yourself rest in awareness-openness, also called awareness-emptiness, without any sense of someone doing anything, something that was done, or anyone to receive. This is called resting in the emptiness of the three spheres, and it can also be repeated after Dedicating (see step 8). The love and compassion that have arisen in your meditation can now move beyond apparent subject-object duality into nonreferential love and compassion.

This interplay between form and emptiness loosens our fixation on being a "helper." In formlessness, we are relieved of having to *be* someone. Rather, we can let go of any identity whatsoever. This can bring relief at not having to be or do something. It can also bring up resistance or anxiety. We are used to hanging on to an idea of who we are. We have worked hard to become a somebody, someone of value and importance. As we become more used to letting go into awareness itself, our consciousness expands and lets go into the vast, unlimited openness. This is the doorway into who we truly are, that which is beyond our changing form, roles, activities, thoughts, and concepts of who we are. The gifts that come to us from an open heart are inexhaustible. This openness-emptiness gives space for insights to arise and blessings to come. The life force in the core of our being can recharge and nourish us.

If we don't cling to our experience, resting in formlessness helps dissolve our self-clinging — our core fixation, the primary cause of our suffering. The union of form and openness in the main part of the meditation dissolves into changeless true nature, without form. Rest without thoughts — rest in aware, lucid clarity, inseparable from openness.

Issues That Can Arise in Dissolving

Dissolving can bring on the fear of becoming nothing. This may lead you to feel that you don't want to let go of form, of your identity. Even though the first step in the meditation is resting in formless awareness, this anxiety doesn't usually come up then. But sometimes it does after doing a meditation with form. You can reassure yourself that *nothing happens*. Our bodies do not go anywhere. Only our attachment to our body loosens. And as I mention earlier, letting our body dissolve into space trains us to be familiar and comfortable with the afterlife, when we do not have a body.

167

COMPLETE MEDITATION
Step 7: Dissolving

Let yourself as Chenrezig dissolve into the vajra in your heart. The vajra shines even more brilliantly. Then let the vajra dissolve from the top and bottom into a point of brilliant white light. Then this drop of light dissolves into space, into formlessness.

Let go of all thoughts, all conceptuality, all sense of a reference point. Let go into open awareness and rest right there. Rest in awareness naturally, your mind inseparable from space, from openness. Rest like this for a few moments or as long as you like.

ON-THE-SPOT MEDITATION
Step 7: Dissolving

Resting our mind inseparable from awareness returns us to step 1. We begin and end in formless awareness. You can do this On-the-Spot version anytime to let go of the intensity of your emotions or thoughts, to let go of emotional volatility, to relax and refresh. Doing this again and again throughout the day is very advantageous. Let go into pure being, into true nature.

Let everything, inside and outside, dissolve into space, into formlessness. Let go into open awareness and rest right there. Rest in awareness naturally, your mind inseparable from space, from openness.

STEP 8

Dedicating

W hen you have finished step 7 and are ready to move on, or if you find your conceptual mind arising again, once more imagine yourself as Chenrezig, and imagine all beings as Chenrezig, as enlightened manifestations of love. This creates what the tradition calls auspicious interdependent causation, *tendril* in Tibetan. In other words, it creates auspicious karma for yourself and all beings to awaken. By envisioning, we open a pathway for this to come into being.

Then, offer any and all benefit from your meditation to all sentient beings everywhere, that all may be fully liberated and fully awakened. This is called dedicating the merit of our spiritual practice. This helps us let go of clinging to self and firmly establishes altruistic intent, the bodhisattva motivation, in our streams of being. You can phrase this dedication using your own words or recite one of the traditional prayers at the end of this step.

In Tibetan Buddhism, there is always a dedication of merit at the conclusion of a meditation. When I first met Kalu

171

Rinpoche in 1977, I did a meditation from this tradition that had a dedication prayer at its conclusion. It was the first time I had ever done this. After a few days, I noticed that dedicating in this way made me feel lighter. My meditation felt empowered. It felt like there was a wind in my sails. Something about not doing my meditation just for my own little self opened everything up. It felt more easeful. I felt less resistance to getting on the cushion and staying with my meditation.

An additional practice is to offer everything we do for the benefit of all beings. In the morning we can pray that everything we do today will benefit all beings. At night we can also dedicate all our activities of the day to all beings. This facilitates us becoming a conduit of awakened activity and an instrument of love. It reminds us of our interconnectedness with everyone and everything. It puts us in the stream of blessing, inseparable from it.

Integrating a Dedication into Moment-to-Moment Life

You can spontaneously create your own dedication at any time, using it as you like. You can also write dedications that you can use whenever you want. We can dedicate our work, our joy, our love, any part of us, or anything we do.

For instance, in step 6, I mentioned my friend Susan Shannon, who counsels death-row inmates. One of her clients has adopted dedication as one of his main spiritual practices. He told her: "I do this every day in my own way. When I work out in my cell, doing burpees, I have a sheet of paper on my wall listing out who I am doing each set for: The first set is for my homeboys; the second is for everyone in rival gangs who are different races; then my family and friends; then all the innocent people; then the plants and animals; then the guys in here — and the list goes on and on. In this way, they all motivate me to stay healthy and dedicate my fitness to them. As I put on my shirt, I think of all the people who have no shirt; same with my pants, my socks, my shoes. I imagine them all there in front of me and imagine them having clothes. Of course, they probably wouldn't want my clothes, but I do it anyway."

This man has been studying Buddhism and meditating for years while in prison. When Susan asked him if he had noticed any changes in his life since he began this practice, he said, "Oh yeah. I am so blessed. I am at peace. I am kind. I haven't cussed in seventeen years. I have good friends, both inside and out." Then he added that since they had been meeting, he had noticed he was getting more calm and peaceful. Not only that, but his reverence for life had changed. Now, if a fly or a spider came into his cell, instead of flushing it or outright killing it, he wants to protect it. He doesn't want to hurt or cause pain to anything for the rest of his life, and this sudden change is stunningly unarguable to him. Susan sees evidence every day at San Quentin that it is possible for hearts to open, for these prisoners to feel regret and to reform.*

Another option, done after Dedicating, is a brief meditation with three steps. It is usually done while ringing a meditation bell once for each step. It is a meditation of letting go completely into emptiness, into shunyata. The first step is to let go of thinking or feeling that there is anyone who did anything in your meditation. In other words, let go of thinking there was a meditator. The second step is to let go of the idea that there

173

---

*   To learn more about Susan Shannon's prison ministry to death-row inmates, visit her website Chaplain of the Heart (http://chaplainof theheart.com).

was anything to give, or that anything was passed from you to another person. The third step is to let go of thinking and feeling that there was anyone who received anything.

This pith meditation is called resting in the emptiness of the three spheres — emptiness of self, emptiness of other, and the emptiness of anything to pass between these two. This is called "sealing your meditation with shunyata." It reminds us that we are all in the dance of illusion. It is a balancing for all our meditations. Doing our meditation we have, subtly or not so subtly, created an identity as a meditator. This last optional step dismantles the tendency for us to do so. It reminds us to rest in the union of the two truths. This meditation integrates the union of emptiness and love, nonduality and love.

174

Traditional Dedication Prayers

I offer these four traditional dedication prayers to you. You can use one or more of these for your dedication. As I mention above, you can create your own On-the-Spot dedication prayers at any moment. In the Tibetan tradition, prayers and aspirations are considered to be very powerful.

Here are the first two:

Through this goodness may awakening spontaneously
arise in our streams of being,
May all obscurations and distortions fall away.
May all beings be liberated from the stormy waves
of birth, old age, sickness, and death.

For the benefit of beings without exception,
I dedicate without any reticence whatsoever,
All the merit accrued through various virtuous acts,
To the incomparable expanse of totality.

These last two dedication prayers are favorites of ours at Sukhasiddhi Foundation, the Tibetan Buddhist center I founded twenty-one years ago. They come from Lex Hixon's book *Mother of the Buddhas: Meditation on the Prajnaparamita Sutra.*[*]

We now intensely cultivate universal love, wishing for all sentient beings only true happiness, fulfillment, peace, and freedom from suffering. We experience great ecstatic joy at the very thought of conscious beings abiding forever in equanimity and bliss, free from every obvious fear and subtle anxiety. As universal love increases in our mind streams, harmful forces cannot affect us, and we become protectors of living beings.

We deeply rejoice in all authentic religious and moral teachings which have elevated any person into selfless love. We rejoice as well in any kind actions performed by, or for, even the least evolved sentient being. We remember constantly that all societies and relationships, in order to be fruitful, can be based upon and sustained by loving-kindness alone.

175

The supremely subtle innate mind of clear light[†] is all goodness. It has no beginning or end. It constantly emanates the dance of compassion and wisdom, performed by oceans of awakened ones and their daughters and sons who pervade innumerable dimensions.

---

[*]   Lex Hixon wrote these prayers using the words of the current Dalai Lama. Small changes have been made.

[†]   This phrase refers to the buddha or awake nature at our core: clarity, luminosity, and emptiness.

May I ripen limitless numbers of transmigrators* in this profound realization.

Abiding in the primordial peace of the natural purity of all phenomena, a fortunate one am I who seeks great bliss. May I be a vessel for the nectar of Dharma, to help all beings, in all worlds, in all ways.[23]

---

* This refers to those who migrate through *samsara*, that is, unawakened mind and its worlds.

COMPLETE MEDITATION
Step 8: Dedicating

Reappear as Chenrezig. This creates auspicious interdependent connections for you to awaken and benefit many beings.

Dedicate any and all benefit of your meditation to the happiness and liberation of all beings. Use your own wording, or use one or both of these two traditional prayers:

> *Through this goodness may awakening spontaneously*
> *arise in our streams of being,*
> *May all obscurations and distortions fall away.*
> *May all beings be liberated from the stormy waves*
> *of birth, old age, sickness, and death.*

And:

> *For the benefit of beings without exception,*
> *I dedicate without any reticence whatsoever,*
> *All the merit accrued through various virtuous acts,*
> *To the incomparable expanse of totality.*

ON-THE-SPOT MEDITATION
Step 8: Dedicating

Dedicating benefit to others helps release my subtle grasping at self. It feels good, like when I cook and share a delicious meal with others. You can do an On-the-Spot dedication after each step of Love on Every Breath, along with the full dedication at the conclusion of the complete meditation.

Dedicate any and all benefit of your meditation to the happiness and liberation of all beings. You may include anything you want in your dedication, such as *May all hunger and poverty be eliminated* or *May peace pervade the world.*

Love on Every Breath for Activists and Those of Other Traditions

*Theologians may quarrel, but the mystics of the world
speak the same language.*

— MEISTER ECKHART

*T*he Love on Every Breath meditation can be adapted so
that it is accessible to anyone and can be used by people from all different backgrounds. Some people may not feel
comfortable with Buddhist imagery or with divine imagery
at all. Some people may prefer a secular approach. However,
people from any spiritual or faith tradition, or those who
are not religious, can successfully modify the Love on Every
Breath meditation to their needs. This section offers options
for doing so.

The underlying principles of Love on Every Breath work
with all spiritual traditions. Step-by-step, these principles are
as follows:

1. Resting in openness with the totality of what is, however we conceive of that; for example, resting in openness in the heart of God.

2. Seeking spiritual sanctuary or refuge.

3. Cultivating an altruistic intention that all beings may benefit from our spiritual practice and all our activities.

4. Seeking to embody universal and unconditional love. Opening into feeling this kind of love.

5. Bringing love and awareness to meet our personal suffering, and transforming that suffering with compassion and love.

6. Bringing compassion and love to meet and transform the suffering of everyone, all beings. This includes loved ones, family, friends, and acquaintances as well as strangers and people who are difficult or challenging.

7. Letting everybody, including ourselves, dissolve into formless presence and rest in open awareness (as in step 1).

8. Dedicating any and all benefit from our spiritual practice to the happiness and well-being of all beings.

Sometimes spiritual practices across traditions are similar. The Native Americans in British Columbia have a smoke-offering ceremony like the Tibetan Rio Sang Chöd (which I mention in steps 3 and 6). After Kalu Rinpoche's Tibetan Buddhist group, Kagyu Kunkhyab Chuling, bought retreat land on Salt Spring Island, near Vancouver, His Holiness the Sixteenth Karmapa was invited to visit and bless the place. He told his Buddhist students that the whole area is under the protection of a local fire god, and he wanted to meet with the local shaman of the tribe native to the area. Tibetan Buddhists have the custom of requesting permission from the local gods or spirits to use their land before they create a new retreat center, monastic institution, or temple. The head medicine man came to the land, met Karmapa, and gave his blessing for the project. Karmapa did a ceremonial request for us to use the land for retreat, and with the shaman, he conducted the Rio Sang Chöd ceremony and its local Native American equivalent. This is a way of acknowledging the local spirits, giving them a smoke offering of juniper, cedar, and sage. When I arrived on the retreat land, it was heartwarming for me to hear that these two traditions had come together to do ceremony.

181

All Religions Come from Awakened Mind

Every talk I heard Kalu Rinpoche give in the last few years of his life included the teaching, "In their essence, all religions come from awakened mind, awakened compassion. They all manifested from wisdom and love." All the world's great spiritual traditions teach followers to cultivate and act out of love and compassion. Love on Every Breath is a tried-and-true method for this purpose that can be adapted to suit your beliefs or perspective.

Kalu Rinpoche was raised by parents who were meditators and who spent much of their time in retreat. At an early age, he was recognized as an incarnation of one of the greatest nineteenth-century Tibetan masters, Jamgon Kongtrul Lodro Thaye. However, his father did not want to have him formally enthroned, so his parents did not send him to the monastery, Palpung in eastern Tibet, until he was about fourteen years old. He was already well trained for his age when he finally arrived, and then he went on to do long retreats there. Later he meditated on his own in caves in the high mountains of Tibet for thirteen years. He only left the caves when his teacher made it plain that it was time to teach in order to benefit people directly. When he was in his midtwenties, he read the Bible in the Tibetan translation. He was considered one of the preeminent Tibetan masters of the twentieth century. Requested by the Bhutanese king in the 1950s, he came and trained lamas in Bhutan for twelve years in the monastery and long retreats. He then moved to Darjeeling, India, and a Gelugpa Rinpoche gave him a small monastery south of town.

During Kalu Rinpoche's years in Darjeeling, he had many Catholic priests come to him for discussions and teachings. He adapted meditations for them. He also interacted with others of various faiths in interfaith gatherings, as a guide or supplementary teacher. In 1971, following requests from the sixteenth Karmapa and the Dalai Lama, he made his first visit to the West. Understanding that the majority of people in the West were Christians, and having reverence for all religious traditions, he made his first stop in Rome, where he went to the Vatican to pay homage to the Pope. He was received graciously by Pope Paul VI. He then went on to Jerusalem to pay homage there.

One day, when I was staying at Rinpoche's monastery, we were in his sitting room where he usually gave teachings, and a group of Jesuit priests came in from Canada. After welcoming them in fellowship, he pulled a rosary out from a little drawer in the table in front of him, indicative of his friendship with Catholic priests. After showing it to the priests, they chatted through the translator for some time. This was not their first visit to see him. Then Rinpoche asked them,

"You have a perfectly good religion. Why do you come to me, an old Tibetan Buddhist?" One of the priests replied, "We do have a wonderful religion, but we need someone to study with." After a little discussion, Rinpoche gave them an adapted meditation on Chenrezig that we all did together.

Recently, I heard a story from a French Buddhist who knew Kalu Rinpoche. The Frenchman told me that he was on expeditions around the French countryside with Kalu Rinpoche back in the midseventies to look for property for a retreat center. At one point, they came to look at a Catholic monastery for sale. It was empty and not in use any longer. The Westerners with Rinpoche thought this place would be perfect, but Rinpoche said, "No. We will not try to buy this place." They questioned him as to why not. He replied, "This land and these buildings should be revitalized and used again for the Catholics." Right then and there, he sat on the ground and proceeded to make prayers for this to happen. Interestingly, it was later taken off the market, and it did end up once again becoming a vital, active place for Catholics.

I love all the authentic spiritual traditions from around the world. When I was nine, my grandmother gave me two tiny books for Christmas. They were called *Occidental Wisdom* and *Oriental Wisdom*. I adored these books. They contained profound quotes from various people and scriptures. I read them every night for years. This was the beginning of my education on other religions and perspectives. Then, when I was a freshman in high school, we studied *The Religions of Man* by Huston Smith, which was a groundbreaking book at the time. I love the richness of the tapestry of our human spiritual teachings. It is like we have a garden with many flowers. Who wants a garden with only one type of flowers, when we can have a variety? Later in college, I went into comparative mysticism. Of course, I had to make this field up and then go for it. My actual degree was in the humanities. In the last ten years I have been honored to be a part of the Contemplative Alliance, a branch of the Global Peace Initiative of Women. We meet in various places around the world to share prayers and meditations from our traditions and to discuss the current global issues we face as human beings. This brings us together in our diversity to hear one another from a place of deep listening and to contemplate what actions we can do alone and together.

A Meditation for Activists and Secular Humanists

The Love on Every Breath meditation can be a very valuable resource for activists, atheists, secular humanists, and nonreligious people. At root, the meditation cultivates benevolent values of healing, happiness, and service; it encourages a very deep caring for others, ourselves, and all beings, regardless of race or creed or even species. You don't need to be Buddhist or even spiritual to benefit from it.

Many people who are committed to and work for truth, justice, equality, and freedom, whether as activists or in other helping professions, will find this meditation calls forth and promotes the highest good for human beings, for animal welfare, and for our planet. This kind of service for humanity can bring happiness, joy, and community and be very rewarding, doing good work for its own sake. When victories are achieved, it often can give our life purpose and meaning. On the other hand, a path of service can also be discouraging and overwhelming at times; it can leave us feeling depleted, burned-out, or angry. It can take everything and more than we have to give. In these situations, Love on Every Breath can nourish and sustain us, giving us renewed energy. It can help us to remember why we are working so hard in the first place. It can help us stay true to our values and get in touch with our heart's deepest truth. It is my hope that you will take this meditation and make it yours, utilizing this ancient meditation to enhance your sense of well-being, your capacity to love, and your effectiveness in the world.

Adapting the Meditation Steps for Other Traditions

What follows are suggestions for adapting the eight meditation steps for other traditions. However, substitutions that are appropriate for your spiritual sensibilities can be made for any aspect of the meditation.

185

Step 1: Resting in Open Awareness

Step 1 is the same for everyone, regardless of beliefs or perspectives. Resting in openness; letting go of preferences, opinions, and ego perspective — all of this is essential, regardless of your spiritual path. This is also a step of letting go into humility. After we let go, we can open to that which is beyond our little self. There can be a sense of freshness, of space, or of possibility. It is hard, if not impossible, to grow spiritually if we are attached to our ideas or if we think that we know everything. So in this step, we let all conceptuality go.

Step 2: Seeking Refuge in Awakened Sanctuary

For those of a different tradition or who want to create their own refuge, consider who or what epitomizes for you the essence of truth and goodness. In Tibetan Buddhism, the union of truth, wisdom, and love, which are formless, is often personified in order to help us more easily make a felt connection. But you do not have to personify these attributes if it doesn't suit you.

If personification helps, focus on a concept or deity that relates to your beliefs. For example, you can substitute God, the Holy Trinity, Jesus, or Mary if you are Christian. Muslims can call on Allah or Muhammad; Jews on the nameless God or the Shekinah; and Hindus on Brahma, Vishnu, Shiva, or one of the other Hindu goddesses or gods. Native peoples can name someone from their own culture, such as the Great Spirit or Wakan Tanka. Taoists might seek refuge from the Celestial Masters or the Tao itself. You might prefer to seek refuge in the Goddess, Gaia, or Mother Earth.

In the Vajrayana refuge meditation, step 2 evokes the "three jewels" and the "three roots," which include various kinds of awakened beings. Each demonstrates various aspects of awakened presence and benefits us in specific ways. If you like, you can look for similar aspects in your tradition. For example, in Hinduism, Shiva has particular traits and attributes that differ from Lakshmi's. The prophets from the Abrahamic traditions vary in their qualities, as do the Christian saints and the sages of various spiritual traditions. You may have some favorites. Hindus look to Yogananda, Nisargadatta, Ramana Maharshi, and many others, depending on whom the individual feels connection with. The sages and saints stand in front of us forming a line or a lineage of support, our spiritual ancestors.

Step 3: Cultivating Awakened Mind

Step 3 is also much the same for everyone. Regardless of the fact that there are Buddhist formulations available for this, the aim is simply to cultivate real altruism within our hearts, a desire to help others. Repeating the traditional prayer is not necessary, though if you find saying a prayer is helpful, adjust the wording to fit your tradition. The important point is expressing and cultivating the altruistic intention that all beings are free of suffering and become established in happiness.

Step 4: Stepping into Love

In step 4, the idea is to open to our innate love and compassion and then to further cultivate it. It is easier for us to think that others are awakened and have infinite, unconditional love, like holy saints or great yogis, rather than ourselves. Our awakened nature, the divine spark at the core of who we are, is the wish-fulfilling jewel that is, in Jesus's words, "the kingdom of heaven within." It is what ultimately brings us to complete contentment, peace, and joy. This is what we are discovering and tending to in ourselves.

187

This ancient Buddhist meditation is a skillful method to help us open to our divine spark and to the depth of love and compassion in ourselves. As in step 2 above, simply imagine the personification, the deity, or your feeling of God, as you know him/her. As I caution in the main meditation, using a human being for this visualization can backfire, since no human is perfect, and the person you choose might one day disappoint or betray you. For this reason, traditionally we use an exemplary awakened being or divine being who cannot disappoint us.

As in the original step 4 instructions, visualize the sacred presence above your head, and open into feeling their love and compassion. Either silently or out loud, express the aspiration or prayer that you might fully and completely embody unconditional love. As a response to your prayer, imagine their transmission and blessing of wisdom-love coming into you. We might need to open again and again to feel the transmission and blessing. At first, this might feel like only our imagination, but over time it becomes an actual felt experience. Then, imagine God or the divine being dissolving into light and into you. Feel your inseparability, your oneness with the pure presence of wisdom and love. This simultaneously appears as a drop of brilliant light or as the crystal vajra in your heart center.

At this point in the meditation, once we have a sense of union with the sacred presence, we traditionally recite the Bodhisattva of Compassion's mantra, the mantra of love, "*Om mani padme hum.*" Saying a mantra is optional, and you can also substitute a prayer or saying from your own tradition that focuses on love and compassion for all beings. Recite the mantra while radiating light from your heart chakra and feeling compassion for all beings.

188

Steps 5 and 6: Taking and Sending for Yourself and for Others

These stages of the meditation are in a form that is already suitable for everyone, and so they do not need to be adapted. Continue to visualize whatever form you chose in steps 2 and 4 in place of Chenrezig. If at any point you feel ego issues coming up, rest in conscious union with your mentor figure.

Steps 7 and 8: Dissolving and Dedicating

Ending the meditation also does not require any particular changes, as the process is universal and flows from what's been established. However, as before, you can modify the visualizations and final prayers as you wish to suit your tradition.

COMPLETE MEDITATION
Love on Every Breath for Activists and Those of Other Traditions

This is the complete version of the Love on Every Breath meditation adapted for those of other traditions, such as for those from other religious faiths, for secular humanists, and for activists. I have not created On-the-Spot versions of these steps, but feel free to adapt each step in whatever way that fits your needs. You can also modify the On-the-Spot meditations in appendix 2.

Step 1: Resting in Open Awareness

Sit comfortably to meditate, with your back upright. Have your eyes open and slightly downcast. Let go of thoughts of the past, present, and future. When thoughts come up, let them go.

Join with attention with your breath. Bring your attention inward and feel the sensations in your body. Let yourself come fully into contact with yourself, with your body and your emotions. Do not speculate about what is. Simply open to observe, feel, and connect with what is manifesting in the moment. As you continue to connect, breathe into your experience and let your mind settle. Rest in awareness, openness, and sensation inseparable.

When you are ready, allow your awareness to gradually radiate out to include your entire body and what is present around you. Let go into openness. Let the mind be like the sky. Perceptions and thoughts, like birds, do not disturb the sky. The sky does not chase after or judge them. They simply are there, and then they are gone. Let everything be; let the mind rest at ease in openness. Keep consciously breathing into your experience and relaxing, your mind at ease, open, and resting in the vividness of your experience.

Step 2: Seeking Refuge in Awakened Sanctuary

Imagine who or what epitomizes for you the essence of truth and goodness. This can be a divine being — such as God, Allah, Shiva, the Great Spirit, and so on. Or this could be a person, like your spiritual teacher, or the formless presence of wisdom and love. Imagine this being in front of you, and open to their presence as you imagine it would be. Call upon them and ask for their support, guidance, and awakened transmission. Then imagine them responding to you with their great love and wisdom. Gradually, you will come to actually feel their support, wisdom, and love.

Chant your own individualized version of a refuge prayer. Do this as many times as you like. You might invoke your divine being in your own words: "I call upon and take refuge in [name of being]." Or, if you don't wish to specify a being, you might say, "I take refuge in truth. Please be present with me and support me."

Step 3: Cultivating Awakened Mind

Set the feeling and intention that you are not just engaging in this meditation for yourself, but rather on behalf of, and for the benefit of, all sentient beings. Consider the suffering that all beings experience and the fact that awakening is what sets beings free and brings them to lasting happiness and peace. Make your intention of awakening to benefit others and help lead them to genuine freedom, joy, and peace.

If you wish, also chant a prayer or pledge to serve and benefit all beings.

Step 4: Stepping into Love

Call upon and imagine your chosen divine being or wise, loving presence above your head. Aspire or pray to fully embody love and compassion for yourself and all beings and to serve as a vehicle for love, compassion, and healing.

191

In answer to your heartfelt aspirations, your chosen being dissolves into light and into you. Feel that you are now inseparable from divine or awakened love. You appear as a body of light.

Inside your heart center is a crystal vajra of light — the essence of indestructible pure being, divine or awakened love. Contemplate the suffering of all beings, and engender compassion for everyone, including yourself.

Imagine that from the crystal vajra in your heart center, sacred or awakened love and compassion radiates in the form of five-colored or rainbow light to all beings and to your ordinary self. If you wish, also chant your own mantra of compassion as many times as you like, or chant the Buddhist mantra "*Om mani padme hum.*"

Step 5: Taking and Sending for Yourself

To begin, appear as awakened presence, a body of light, the union of all awakened love and compassion, and in your heart, imagine the vajra of crystal light that is the essence of awakened love and wisdom. In the full meditation, this is done in step 4, or you can "flash on" this visualization more quickly.

When this is done, imagine your ordinary human self sitting in front of and facing you.

Get in touch with any aspect of your suffering and open to loving-kindness and compassion for yourself. Work through any issues that arise, such as unworthiness. See your suffering as black smoke, and breathe it into your heart center. As soon as the smoke touches the vajra, let a lightning bolt of brilliant white light transform the suffering into awakened love, compassion, and healing energy. Breathe out this white light, awakened love, into yourself sitting in front of you. Repeat this process again and again, synchronizing the meditation with your breath. Imagine your ordinary self filling with white light, awakened love. This light alleviates suffering and brings about awakening. Imagine yourself becoming gradually healed, illuminated, and awakened.

Occasionally restabilize the sense of yourself as awakened presence, inseparable from your chosen divine being, the saints and the sages, or any other persons or concepts you have invoked.

One option, if you wish, is to modify the meditation like this: After getting in touch with your suffering, consider all the people who suffer with the same or a similar affliction. Then imagine all these people in front of you, surrounding your ordinary self, and visualize taking and sending for the whole group of fellow sufferers, simultaneously with yourself.

Step 6: Taking and Sending for Others

To begin, imagine yourself appearing as a body of light, the union of awakened compassion, and envision a crystal vajra of light in your heart. This is done in step 4, or you can "flash on" this visualization more quickly.

When this is done, see the person or people in front of you whom you want to work with. Contemplate their suffering and open to feel loving-kindness and compassion for them.

As in the previous step, synchronize this visualization with your breath: On the in-breath, breathe in their suffering as black smoke, and see it instantaneously, spontaneously transformed by the lightning bolt emanating from the vajra. This transforms their suffering into white light, awakened compassion, love, and healing energy.

Breathe out this light to the person or people in front of you. Repeat this visualization until you see them filling with light, becoming healed, happy, and awakened.

Occasionally restabilize the sense of yourself as awakened presence, inseparable from your chosen divine being, the saints and the sages, wisdom, and love.

Gradually extend your Love on Every Breath meditation to include all beings, imagining them in front of you. Finally, imagine everyone filled with white light, healed, liberated, and completely awakened. Rest in this.

For a very brief version:
Breathe into suffering. See and feel it being transformed by the crystal vajra and the lightning bolt of enlightened heart-mind. Breathe out love to yourself and all beings, to the entirety of what is.

Step 7: Dissolving

Let all that you have engaged with, yourself as awakened presence, the vajra in your heart, thoughts and feelings of compassion — let it all dissolve into space, into formlessness.

Let go of all thoughts, all conceptuality, all sense of a reference point. Let go into open awareness and rest right there. Rest in awareness naturally, your mind inseparable from space, from openness. Rest like this for a few moments or as long as you like.

Step 8: Dedicating

Dedicate any and all benefit of your meditation to the happiness and liberation of all beings. For example, you may use this prayer or create one of your own:

May any and all benefit arising from my meditation be dedicated to the well-being, happiness, and liberation of all beings. May we all come to live in harmony, peace, and joy.

Complete Traditional Meditation

Step 1: Resting in Open Awareness

Sit comfortably to meditate, with your back upright. Have your eyes open and slightly downcast. Let go of thoughts of the past, present, and future. When thoughts arise again, let go of them, again and again.

Join your attention with your breath. Bring your attention inward and feel the sensations in your body. Let yourself come fully into contact with yourself, with your body and your emotions. Do not speculate about what is. Simply open to observe, feel, and connect with what is manifesting in the moment. As you continue to connect, breathe into your experience and let your mind settle. Rest in awareness, openness, and sensation inseparable.

When you are ready, allow your awareness to gradually radiate out to include your entire body and what is present around you. Let go into openness. Let the mind be like the sky. Perceptions and thoughts, like birds, do not disturb the sky. The sky does not chase after or judge them. They simply are there, and then they are gone. Let everything be; let the mind rest at ease in openness. Keep consciously breathing into your experience and relaxing, keeping your mind at ease, open, and resting in the vividness of your experience.

Step 2: Seeking Refuge in Awakened Sanctuary

Call upon the Buddha, the Dharma, and the Noble Sangha. See them appear in the sky in front of you. Ask for their support, guidance, and awakened transmission. Open to their presence, and imagine them responding to you with their great love and wisdom. Gradually, you will come to actually find sanctuary in their support, wisdom, and love.

Chant this refuge prayer three or seven times:

> *Until awakening I take refuge in the Buddha,*
> *the Dharma, and the Noble Sangha,*
> *By the merit of my acts of generosity and other*
> *awakening qualities,*
> *May I attain full awakening for the benefit of all beings.*

Or, if you wish, for the full Vajrayana version, in addition to the above, also call upon the gurus, the *yidams*, the dakas, the dakinis, and the protectors, and chant the following prayer:

> *I go for refuge to the glorious holy gurus.*
> *I go for refuge to the buddhas, the transcendent conquerors.*
> *I go for refuge to the sacred Dharma.*
> *I go for refuge to the Noble Sangha.*
> *I go for refuge to the assembly of dakas, dakinis, Dharma*
> *protectors, and guardians, all who possess the eye of*
> *awakened awareness.*

The enlightened beings dissolve into you. You become inseparable from them. Feel their blessing. Then let go and rest again in formlessness.

Step 3: Cultivating Awakened Mind

Set the feeling and intention that you are not just engaging in this meditation for yourself, but rather on behalf of, and for the benefit of, all sentient beings. Consider the suffering that all beings experience and the fact that awakening is what sets beings free and brings them lasting happiness and peace. Make your intention of awakening to benefit others and help lead them to genuine freedom, joy, and peace.

Then chant this prayer (which is also chanted in step 2):

197

> *Until awakening I take refuge in the Buddha,*
> *the Dharma, and the Noble Sangha,*
> *By the merit of my acts of generosity and other*
> *awakening qualities,*
> *May I attain full awakening for the benefit of all beings.*

Or chant the following prayer:

> *Just as the buddhas of the past aroused their altruistic awakened mind and applied themselves step-by-step to the training of a bodhisattva, so, too, in order to serve beings, I arouse my bodhicitta motivation and will pursue the training step-by-step.*

Step 4: Stepping into Love

Call upon and imagine Chenrezig above your head. Aspire and pray to fully embody love and compassion for yourself and all beings and serve as a vehicle for healing.

In answer to your heartfelt aspirations, Chenrezig dissolves into light and into you. Feel that you are now inseparable from awakened body, speech, and mind, and especially from the love of the Bodhisattva of Compassion, who embodies the love of all the buddhas and bodhisattvas. You then appear in the form of Chenrezig, a body of light.

Inside your heart chakra is a crystal vajra of light — the essence of indestructible pure being, awakened love. If you wish, expand this visualization to include a small Chenrezig sitting on a lotus and moon seat in your heart, and inside Chenrezig's heart is the crystal vajra of light. Contemplate the suffering of all beings, and engender compassion for everyone, including yourself.

From the vajra, radiate love in the form of five-colored light to all beings and to your ordinary self. If you wish, chant, out loud or silently, the powerful mantra "*Om mani padme hum.*" Chant as long as you like, but traditionally in Buddhism, chanting 3, 7, 21, or 108 times is considered auspicious.

Step 5: Taking and Sending for Yourself

To begin, imagine yourself as Chenrezig, enlightened being, the union of all awakened love and compassion, and in your heart chakra, imagine a vajra of crystal light that is the essence of awakened love and wisdom. If you like, you may see the vajra inside a tiny Chenrezig's heart. As many times as you wish, chant the mantra "*Om mani padme hum.*"

When this is done, imagine your ordinary human self sitting in front of and facing you.

Get in touch with any aspect of your suffering and open to loving-kindness and compassion for yourself. Work through any issues that arise, such as unworthiness. See your suffering as black smoke, and breathe it into your heart chakra. As soon as the smoke touches the vajra, let a lightning bolt of brilliant white light transform the suffering into awakened love, compassion, and healing energy. Breathe out this white light, awakened love, into yourself sitting in front of you. Repeat this process again and again, synchronizing the meditation with your breath. Imagine your ordinary self filling with white light, which is awakened love. This light alleviates suffering and brings about awakening. Imagine yourself becoming gradually healed, illuminated, and awakened.

Occasionally restabilize the sense of yourself as awakened presence, as the awakened Bodhisattva of Compassion inseparable from the presence, wisdom, and love of all the enlightened ones.

One option, if you wish, is to modify the meditation like this: After getting in touch with one aspect of your suffering, consider all the people who suffer with the same or a similar affliction. For example, think: *Oh, just like me, many people suffer from headaches! By my suffering this headache, may all those suffering from headaches be freed from this pain.* Then imagine all these people in front of you, surrounding your ordinary self. Imagine your own and everyone's suffering as black smoke, and imagine that your own and everyone's suffering, simultaneously and at once, is transformed by the vajra.

Step 6: Taking and Sending for Others

To begin, imagine yourself as Chenrezig, enlightened being, the union of all awakened love and compassion, and in your heart chakra, imagine a vajra of crystal light that is the essence of awakened love and wisdom. If you like, you may see the vajra inside a tiny Chenrezig's heart. As many times as you wish, chant the mantra "*Om mani padme hum.*"

When this is done, see the person or people in front of you whom you want to work with. Contemplate their suffering and open to feel loving-kindness and compassion for them.

Synchronize this visualization with your breath: On the in-breath, breathe in their suffering as black smoke, and see it instantaneously, spontaneously transformed by the lightning bolt emanating from the vajra. This transforms their suffering into white light, awakened compassion, love, and healing energy.

Breathe out this light into the person or people in front of you. Repeat this visualization until you see them filling with light, being healed, happy, and awakened.

Occasionally restabilize the sense of yourself as awakened presence, as the awakened Bodhisattva of Compassion inseparable from wisdom and love. If you like, repeat the mantra "*Om mani padme hum*" for a time.

Gradually extend your Love on Every Breath meditation to include all beings, imagining them in front of you. Finally, imagine everyone filled with white light, healed, liberated, and completely awakened. Rest in this.

Step 7: Dissolving

Let yourself as Chenrezig dissolve into the vajra in your heart. The vajra shines even more brilliantly. Then let the vajra dissolve from the top and bottom into a point of brilliant white light. Then this drop of light dissolves into space, into formlessness.

Let go of all thoughts, all conceptuality, all sense of a reference point. Let go into open awareness and rest right there. Rest in awareness naturally, your mind inseparable from space, from openness. Rest like this for a few moments or as long as you like.

Step 8: Dedicating

Reappear as Chenrezig. This creates auspicious interdependent connections for you to awaken and benefit many beings.

Dedicate any and all benefit of your meditation to the happiness and liberation of all beings. Use your own wording, or use one or both of these two traditional prayers:

> *Through this goodness may awakening spontaneously*
> *arise in our streams of being,*
> *May all obscurations and distortions fall away.*
> *May all beings be liberated from the stormy waves*
> *of birth, old age, sickness, and death.*

And:

> *For the benefit of beings without exception,*
> *I dedicate without any reticence whatsoever,*
> *All the merit accrued through various virtuous acts,*
> *To the incomparable expanse of totality.*

Complete On-the-Spot Meditation

Each of these steps can be done by itself in a few moments at any time during the course of daily life. While doing the entire meditation at once is usually the most powerful, it is also very transformative to do a thirty-second or two- to three-minute meditation. Once you are familiar with the steps, you can instantly call them to mind; these On-the-Spot versions are meant to help you with this. Of course, while the phrasing is short, you can take as long as you like to do a step. These are yours to use anytime, anywhere, as part of your ongoing or daily meditation practice.

Step 1: Resting in Open Awareness

Let go of thoughts. Let everything be as it is. Let the mind rest at ease in openness. When thoughts arise, let go of them, again and again.

Keep consciously breathing into your experience and relaxing, keeping your mind at ease, open, and focusing on stillness and the vividness of your experience.

Step 2: Seeking Refuge in Awakened Sanctuary

Call upon the Buddha, the Dharma, and the Noble Sangha. Ask for their support and guidance. Imagine them in front of you, responding with their great love and wisdom. Gradually, you will come to actually feel sanctuary in their support, wisdom, and love.

Pray to these beings for sanctuary. Open to a sense of connection and transmission from awakened presence.

The refuge beings dissolve into you, and you become inseparable from them. You and all that is dissolve into open space. Rest your mind in evenness, inseparable from openness.

Step 3: Cultivating Awakened Mind

Cultivate the wish to fully awaken in order to completely free others and yourself from suffering and to establish everyone in complete freedom, joy, and peace.

Step 4: Stepping into Love

Feel that you are inseparable from awakened compassion and love, and appear as Chenrezig. Or simply see yourself in your ordinary form, filled with blessing and love.

A crystal vajra of light in your heart radiates love as light out to one being, several, or all beings.

Simultaneously, if you like, chant the mantra of compassion and love, "*Om mani padme hum.*"

Step 5: Taking and Sending for Yourself

Imagine your ordinary self in front of and facing you. Open into feeling any suffering that is present in your human self, and open to feel loving-kindness and compassion for yourself.

See your human self's suffering as black smoke, and breathe it into the vajra in your heart chakra. As soon as it touches the vajra, a lightning bolt emerges from the vajra, instantly transforming the suffering into white light that is awakened love and healing energy.

Breathe out the transformed energy as white light into your human self in front of you. See the white light filling your ordinary self, bringing healing and awakening. See yourself as healed, awakened.

Repeat this, for as long as you like, synchronizing the visualization with the breath.

One option, if you wish, is this modification: After contemplating your suffering, think about all those who are suffering in a similar way, and think, for example: *Oh, just like me, many people suffer from headaches! By my suffering this headache, may all those suffering from this be freed from this pain.* Then imagine all these people in front of you, surrounding your ordinary self, and do the Taking and Sending visualization for the whole group simultaneously with yourself.

Step 6: Taking and Sending for Others

Envision a crystal vajra of light in your heart. See the person or people in front of you whom you want to work with. Contemplate their suffering and open to feel loving-kindness and compassion for them.

Breathe in their suffering as black smoke, and see it instantaneously, spontaneously transformed by the lightning bolt emanating from the vajra. This transforms their suffering into white light, awakened compassion, love, and healing energy.

Breathe out this light to the person or people in front of you. See them filling with light, being healed, happy, and awakened.

For an even briefer version:
Breathe into suffering. See and feel it transformed by the crystal vajra and the lightning bolt of enlightened heart-mind. Breathe out love to yourself and all beings, to the entirety of what is.

Step 7: Dissolving

Let everything, inside and outside, dissolve into space, into formlessness. Let go into open awareness and rest right there. Rest in awareness naturally, your mind inseparable from space, from openness.

Step 8: Dedicating

Dedicate any and all benefit of your meditation to the happiness and liberation of all beings. You may include anything you want in your dedication, such as *May all hunger and poverty be eliminated* or *May peace pervade the world.*

Acknowledgments

My undying gratitude and love go to my primary teacher, Kalu Rinpoche. My life changed completely due to his joyful, loving, awakened presence. I had no idea of the love, peace, delight, and liberation that would settle in me from his kindness and teachings. Kalu Rinpoche was first among the Tibetan masters to give us Westerners, scraggly bunch that we were, an opportunity to go into three-year, three-month retreat in order to train deeply in meditation and yoga. He was the first to authorize Westerners as lamas. Rinpoche believed in and trusted us. He told us that we would have to figure out how to teach Dharma for the Westerners, and he gave us the love, support, and skills to do it.

I also want to thank all my other main teachers — His Holiness the Sixteenth Karmapa, Jamgon Kongtrul the Third, Bokar Rinpoche, Situ Rinpoche, Dudjom Rinpoche, Druptop Rinpoche, Dezchung Rinpoche, and Khenpo Tsultrim Gyamtso Rinpoche. Your generosity and love, your wisdom and awakened embodiment, held me, fed me, inspired me, and brought me understanding and realization.

Without the inspiration of my dear friend Lewis Richmond, Zen teacher and author, I would not have written this book. Lew supported me from the beginning, encouraging me to find my voice and share my personal experiences, as well as my understanding of Buddha Dharma.

We enjoyed many delightful conversations envisioning this book into reality.

Thanks to Jason Gardner, my editor, and the team at New World Library, who believed in this book from the beginning! It is a joy to work with you all.

Many supported me in writing this book. My heart overflows with your kindness and love. My daughter, Jessie Wood, contributed her editing skills and supported me when the going got tough. My friend Sylvia Boorstein enthusiastically offered to write the foreword. Thank you to Christine Carter for being a writing buddy extraordinaire.

Matt Spalding and Elise Umansky offered me sanctuary in their guesthouse overlooking the Pacific Ocean. Thanks to Zuleikha Bethami, Sherry Anderson, Roger Housden, Miranda MacPherson, John and Jennifer Welwood, Wendy Garling, Jane Hirschfield, Susan Shannon, Tamam and Shabda Kahn, Alan Giancarlo Alioto, Stina Permild, and Deborah and Jonathon Lewis for the most precious gifts of friendship, loving support, and conversation. Kelly Minor and Carol Aronoff offered editing suggestions. Nancy Sylvester, a Catholic Sister, kindly read the manuscript and offered feedback. Donna Shoemaker gave me nutritional support. Moira Opalka kept my body and soul together with acupuncture. Rachel Chambers brought me delicious home-cooked food and walked my dog when I was tied to my writing seat. Thanks to everyone else who walked Henry, too!

Finally, to all the students and teachers at Sukhasiddhi Foundation who travel with me on the path of awakening. You have been my sustaining inspiration and joy for the last twenty-one years. Thank you for your depth of meditation practice, for sharing your sorrows and joys, and for your love. Watching you all blossom sustains me as a teacher. Lama Drupgyu has been an inestimable help and support with our Sukhasiddhi Sangha and a true Dharma friend. As well, Lamas Dondrup, Annik, Pat, and Stephen covered my teaching, and our board funded my sabbatical, during which I rested up, hiked, and began this book.

Endnotes

1. Roger Walsh, *Essential Spirituality* (New York: John Wiley & Sons, 1999), 72.
2. Lara B. Aknin, J. Kiley Hamlin, and Elizabeth W. Dunn, "Giving Leads to Happiness in Young Children," PLOS/ONE 7, no. 6 (June 14, 2012), e39211, https://doi.org/10.1371/journal.pone .0039211. These researchers investigated whether toddlers under two years of age experienced "greater happiness when giving treats to others rather than receiving treats themselves." With the use of puppets, the children were guided to either play with a toy and the puppet or share a toy with the puppet. They found that children displayed a greater degree of happiness when they shared their toy versus just playing with their toy. In another five-phase experiment, researchers found that the children consistently exhibited a greater degree of happiness giving treats to the puppet than when receiving treats for themselves.

    For more on this, see Maia Szalavitz, "Is Human Nature Fundamentally Selfish or Altruistic?" *Time*, October 8, 2012: In support of altruism being necessary for the survival of communities and civilizations, Szalavitz presents data that shows humans naturally respond to help and give without being asked. See Patricia Kanngiesser and Felix Warneken, "Young Children

Consider Merit When Sharing Resources with Others," PLoS
ONE 7, no. 8 (August 2012), doi:10.1371/journal.pone.0043979: In
this study, children between the ages of three and five were part-
nered and asked to share merit-based rewards with their partner.
Together, the partners were directed to complete a task, and
afterward, the children holding stickers consistently gave their
partner a greater share of stickers when the partner completed
more work on the task, even if it meant keeping fewer stickers for
themselves.

Further, see Eric Michael Johnson, "Ayn Rand vs. the Pyg-
mies: Did Human Evolution Favor Individualists or Altruists?"
Slate, October 3, 2012. Johnson says that Rand's assertion that
"we are rational egotists trapped in a net of social obligations" is
in contrast to human nature. Johnson's study of our earliest civ-
ilizations demonstrates that the evolution of humans consisted
of an increase in community building, and not individualism,
for the survival of civilization. In reports on 150 hunter-gatherer
societies still living as their earliest ancestors did, what was found
was that 100 percent of these societies always favored sharing and
cooperation.

3. The traditional Tibetan prayer is translated by Ken McLeod, with
minor edits by the author.

4. Khenpo Tsultrim Gyamtso, *The Sun of Wisdom,* trans. Ari Gold-
field (Boston: Shambhala, 2003).

5. Jennifer Welwood, "The Jewel Inside," *Poems for the Path*
(self-published, 2001), 17.

6. Dr. Daniel Siegel states, "Our experiences stimulate neural firing
and sculpt our emerging synaptic connections. This is how
experience changes the structure of the brain itself — and could
even end up having an influence on our innate temperament."
See Daniel Siegel, *Mindsight: Transform Your Brain with the New
Science of Kindness* (London: Oneworld Publications, 2011), 42.

7. See Emma M. Seppälä, "Compassion: Our First Instinct," *Psychology Today*, June 3, 2013, https://www.psychologytoday.com/
us/blog/feeling-it/201306/compassion-our-first-instinct; and
Dacher Keltner, Jason Marsh, and Jeremy Adam Smith, eds., *The*

Compassionate Instinct: The Science of Human Goodness.(New York: W. W. Norton, 2010).

8. For more on the brain's pathways, see Rick Hanson, *Buddha's Brain: The Practical Neuroscience of Happiness, Love, and Wisdom* (Oakland, CA: New Harbinger Publications, 2009); Rick Hanson, *Hardwiring Happiness: The New Brain Science of Contentment, Calm, and Confidence* (New York: Harmony, 2013); and John B. Arden, *Rewire Your Brain: Think Your Way to a Better Life* (Hoboken, NJ: John Wiley & Sons, 2010).

9. Roger Housden, *Keeping the Faith Without a Religion* (Boulder, CO: Sounds True, 2014), 2.

10. For more on how helping others leads to happiness, see the HeartMath Institute's article "Altruism: A Remedy for Stress" (www.heartmath.com/blog/articles/altruism-a-remedy -for-stress__trashed). It cites a study that found that high levels of the neurochemical oxytocin, the "love" or "bonding" hormone, were found in people who were very charitable. Dr. Stephen Post, head of the Institute for Research on Unlimited Love, told WebMd: "This is the care-and-connection part of the brain. States of joy and delight come from giving to others. It doesn't come from any dry action...." The Institute of HeartMath studies the physiology of and relationship between the heart, stress, and emotions, and its researchers have found that the heart secretes higher levels of oxytocin when one offers a helping hand to others, in turn relieving stress. Another study that followed over four hundred women for thirty years found that 52 percent who did not volunteer experienced a major illness, compared to 36 percent of those who volunteered.

In addition, see Emiliana Simon-Thomas, "What is the Science of Happiness?" Berkeley Wellness, November 9, 2015, http://www.berkeleywellness.com/healthy-mind/mind-body/ article/what-science-happiness. This article, which presents the results of an ongoing happiness survey, says that the number one thing that makes people happy is strong social connections. This relates to the finding that systems in our bodies are built to be more social, such as the mesolimbic dopamine system, which causes people to feel pleasure when they give to others. In addition, it cites an fMRI study by Bill Harbaugh at the University of Oregon that explored how giving to others generates pleasure. In essence, when volunteers were told the money they were earning would be given to charity, the pleasure centers of the brain lit up the same way they did when the people were told they'd keep their money.

11. David R. Hamilton, "5 Beneficial Side Effects of Kindness," *Huffington Post*, August 2, 2011, https://www.huffpost.com/entry/kindness-benefits_b_869537. This article is based on Hamilton's book *Why Kindness Is Good for You*. It lists five benefits to altruistic kindness: (1) Kindness makes us happier; (2) kindness gives us healthier hearts; (3) kindness slows aging; (4) kindness makes for better relationships; and (5) kindness is contagious. Hamilton asserts, "Oxytocin releases a chemical called nitric oxide (NO) in blood vessels, which dilates (expands) the blood vessels. This reduces blood pressure, and therefore oxytocin is known as a 'cardio-protective' hormone because it protects the heart (by lowering blood pressure)." Ultimately, from reducing inflammation to inspiring others, kindness toward others is healthy.

12. His Holiness the Dalai Lama and Archbishop Desmond Tutu, *The Book of Joy: Lasting Happiness in a Changing World* (New York: Avery, 2016), 59, 61.

13. F. Warneken and M. Tomasello, "The Roots of Human Altruism," *British Journal of Psychology* 100 (August 2009), 455–71, https://www.ncbi.nlm.nih.gov/pubmed/19063815.

14. Shantideva, *The Way of the Bodhisattva: A Translation of the Bodhicharyavatara*, trans. the Padmakara Translation Group (Boston: Shambhala, 1997), 51–52.

15. Hamilton, "5 Beneficial Side Effects of Kindness."

16. Coleman Barks and John Moyne, trans., *The Essential Rumi* (San Francisco: HarperSanFrancisco, 1995/2004), 109.

17. See Daniel Siegel, *Mindsight: Transform Your Brain with the New Science of Kindness* (London: Oneworld Publications, 2011). Dr. Siegel states, "Today we can actually track scientifically the neural dimensions of our narrow definitions of self. When our resonance circuits are engaged, we can feel another's feelings and create a cortical imprint that lets us understand what may be

going on in the other's mind" (page 257). And also: "The study
of positive psychology suggests that being involved in something larger than a personal self creates a sense of meaning and
well-being — an essential part of the experience of 'happiness'"
(page 258). Dr. Siegel asserts that we are built to be a "we."

18. See Seppälä, "Compassion: Our First Instinct." Seppälä states that
studies conducted by Ed Diener and Martin Seligman, leaders in
positive psychology, suggest that when we connect with others in
meaningful ways, we enjoy better mental and physical health and
can experience speedier recovery from disease. Another study
found that people who were happy from living the "good life"
had high levels of inflammation compared to the people whose
happiness derived from living a life of purpose and meaning —
one that focused on others instead of themselves.

19. See Glen Rein, Mike Atkinson, and Rollin McCraty, "The
Physiological and Psychological Effects of Compassion and
Anger," *Journal of Advancement in Medicine* 8, no. 2 (1995). In
the authors' study, thirty participants' heart rate and mood were
measured before and after experiencing care and compassion or
anger and frustration. Specific internal and external techniques
were used to arouse emotional states. By studying immune
system responses, researchers found that participants, after
experiencing anger and frustration, had significantly decreased
immune systems, while after experiencing care and compassion,
they had increased or improved immune system responses.

20. Hamilton, "5 Beneficial Side Effects of Kindness."

21. Thich Nhat Hanh, *Call Me by My True Names* (Berkeley, CA:
Parallax Press, 1999), 72–73.

22. See Melanie Rudd and Jennifer Aaker, "How to Be Happy by
Giving to Others: The Secret of the Helper's High," *Scientific
American*, July 8, 2014, https://www.scientificamerican.com/
article/how-to-be-happy-by-giving-to-others. This article
focuses on Rudd and Aaker's study on how giving increases
happiness. In one exercise, they gave participants twenty-four
hours to perform an act of kindness: Half were asked to make
someone happy; the other half to make someone smile. The
results showed that the concrete instruction of making someone

smile yielded a greater degree of happiness in the participants. In fact, they found across several studies that setting a clear concrete goal, rather than an abstract goal, yielded greater happiness to the giver.

See also Stephen Post, "It's Good to be Good," Stony Brook University News, December 21, 2011, https://news.stonybrook .edu/newsroom/press-release/general/122111stephenpost. Dr. Post writes that in a national survey of 4,582 American adults, "41 percent of Americans volunteered an average of two hours per week; 68 percent of volunteers agree that volunteering 'has made me feel physically healthier'; and 96 percent say volunteering 'makes people happier.'"

23. Lex Hixon, *Mother of the Buddhas: Meditation on the Prajna-paramita Sutra* (Wheaton, IL: Quest Books, 1993), 257, 260. Minor changes in translation made by Lama Thapkhay (Peter Barth).

About the Author

*I*n 1986 Lama Palden Drolma was one of the first Western women to be authorized as a lama, following her completion of the traditional Tibetan three-year, three-month retreat. She has been a student and practitioner of Buddhism and comparative mysticism for over forty years. Her primary teacher was Kalu Rinpoche, and she founded Sukhasiddhi Foundation (www.sukhasiddhi.org) in Marin County, California, to continue his teaching in the Shangpa and Kagyu lineages of Tibetan Buddhism. Lama Palden has a deep interest in helping to make the teachings and practices of Vajrayana Buddhism accessible and practical for Westerners in order to help students actualize our innate wisdom, love, and joy. As a teacher, she is committed to promoting each student's unique unfolding and blossoming.

In 1993 Lama Palden completed a master's degree in counseling psychology at Santa Clara University in Silicon Valley. As a licensed psychotherapist, she facilitates clients' psychospiritual integration and development through bringing together understandings and methods from Buddhism and psychology, as well as from the Diamond Heart work, which she trained in for many years.